U.S. Department of Justice
Office of Justice Programs
Bureau of Justice Statistics

I0448392

Sexual Victimization in Juvenile Facilities Reported by Youth, 2012

National Survey of Youth in Custody, 2012

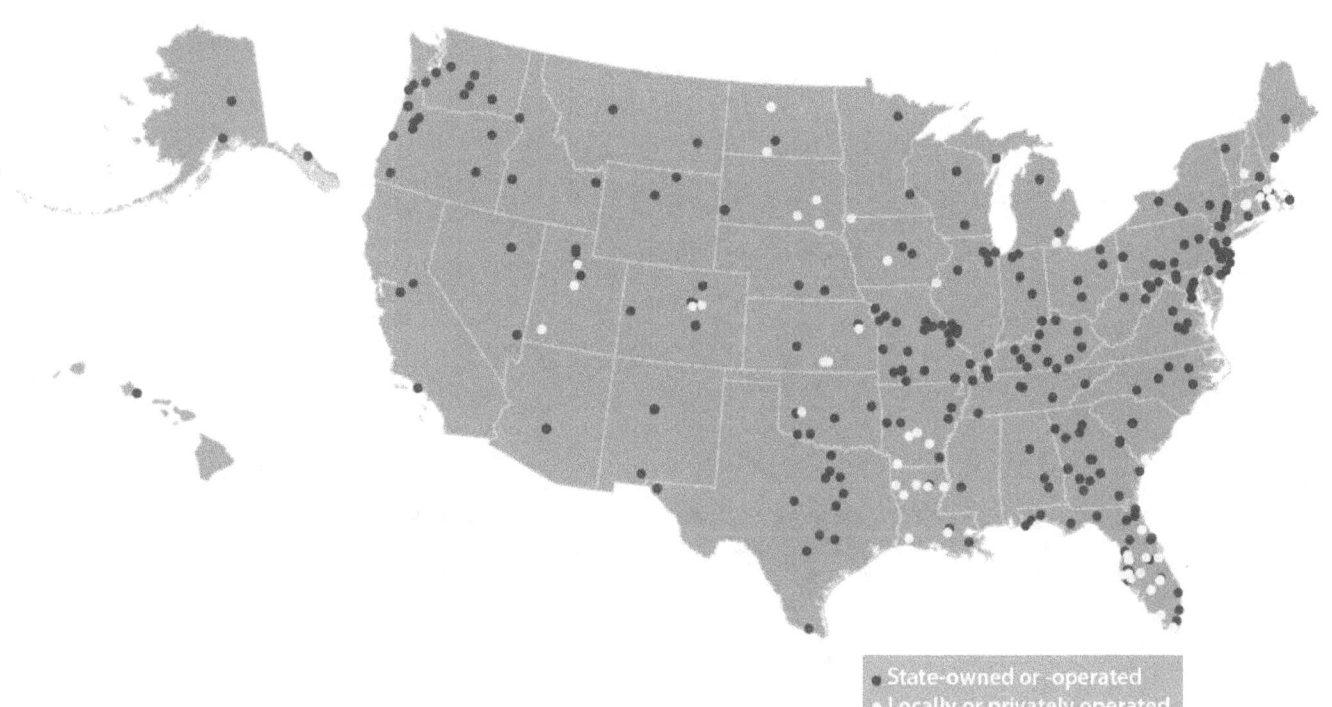

State-owned or -operated
Locally or privately operated

Allen J. Beck, Ph.D.
BJS Statistician

David Cantor, Ph.D., John Hartge, and Tim Smith
Westat

June 2013, NCJ 241708

Bureau of Justice Statistics

William J. Sabol, Ph.D.
Acting Director

BJS Website:

www.bjs.gov
askbjs@usdoj.gov

The Bureau of Justice Statistics is the statistical agency of the U.S. Department of Justice. William J. Sabol is the acting director.

This report was written by Allen J. Beck, Ph.D., BJS Statistician, David Cantor, Ph.D., Westat Vice-President, and John Hartge and Tim Smith, Westat Senior Study Directors.

Paul Guerino (former BJS Statistician), under the supervision of Allen J. Beck, was the project manager for the second National Survey of Youth in Custody. Westat staff, under a cooperative agreement and in collaboration with BJS, designed the survey, developed the questionnaires, coordinated logistical arrangements related to interviewing, collected and processed the data, and assisted in table development. The project team included David Cantor and Andrea Sedlak, Co-Principal Investigators; John Hartge and Tim Smith, Co-Project Directors; Greg Norman, Sampling Statistician; Alfred Bishop, Computer Systems; Susan Cross, Director of Enrollment/Consent Operations; Sherry Sanborne, Field Director; and an extensive project team of researchers, analysts, and programmers. Andrea Burch, BJS Statistician, and Leanne Heaton, Westat Associate Field Director, verified the report.

Morgan Young and Jill Thomas edited the report, and Barbara Quinn designed and produced the report under the supervision of Doris J. James.

June 2013, NCJ 241708

Contents

Highlights 4

National Survey of Youth in Custody-2 6

Prevalence of sexual victimization 9

Facility-level rates 12

State-level rates 18

Demographic and other youth characteristics 20

Circumstances surrounding the incident 21

Methodology 26

Appendix 1. Survey items measuring sexual activity within the facility during the past 12 months or since entering the facility, if less than 12 months 32

Appendix 2. Survey items measuring pressure or nature of coercion . .34

Appendix 3. Items checked for extreme and inconsistent response patterns 35

List of tables

Table 1. Youth reporting sexual victimization, by type of incident, National Survey of Youth in Custody, 2012 9

Table 2. Youth reporting sexual victimization in state juvenile facilities, by type of incident and survey year, National Survey of Youth in Custody, 2008–09 and 2012 10

Table 3. Percent of youth reporting sexual victimization, by youth opinions about facility and staff, facility size, and exposure time, National Survey of Youth in Custody, 2008–09 and 2012 11

Table 4. Juvenile facilities with the highest rates of sexual victimization, National Survey of Youth in Custody, 2012 12

Table 5. Juvenile facilities with the lowest rates of sexual victimization, National Survey of Youth in Custody, 2012 14

Table 6. Juvenile facilities with the highest rates of sexual victimization, by type of contact, National Survey of Youth in Custody, 2012 15

Table 7. Juvenile facilities with the highest rates of sexual victimization, by type of incident, National Survey of Youth in Custody, 2012 16

Table 8. Juvenile facilities with the highest rates of staff sexual victimization, by use of force, National Survey of Youth in Custody, 2012 16

Table 9. Prevalence of sexual victimization, by type of incident and selected facility characteristics, National Survey of Youth in Custody, 2012 17

Table 10. Percent of youth reporting sexual victimization, by state, National Survey of Youth in Custody, 2012 19

Table 11. Prevalence of sexual victimization, by type of incident and selected youth victim characteristics, National Survey of Youth in Custody, 2012 20

Table 12. Experiences of youth-on-youth victims of sexual victimization, National Survey of Youth in Custody, 2012 21

Table 13. Circumstances surrounding youth-on-youth sexual victimization, National Survey of Youth in Custody, 2012 22

Table 14. Victims of staff sexual misconduct, by use of force and sex of youth and staff, National Survey of Youth in Custody, 2012 23

Table 15. Circumstances surrounding incidents of staff sexual misconduct, National Survey of Youth in Custody, 2012 24

Table 16. Victims of staff sexual misconduct, by relationship characteristic, National Survey of Youth in Custody, 2012 25

Table 17. Estimated rates of sexual victimization and lower bounds of the 95%-confidence intervals among high-rate facilities, by exclusion criteria, National Survey of Youth in Custody, 2012 31

List of appendix tables

Appendix table 1. Characteristics of juvenile facilities participating in the National Survey of Youth in Custody, 2012 36

Appendix table 2. Percent of youth reporting sexual victimization, by facility, National Survey of Youth in Custody, 2012 44

Appendix table 3. Percent of youth reporting sexual victimization by another youth, by type of incident and facility, National Survey of Youth in Custody, 2012 48

Appendix table 4. Percent of youth reporting staff sexual misconduct, by type of incident and facility, National Survey of Youth in Custody, 2012 . . .53

Appendix table 5. Percent of youth reporting staff sexual misconduct excluding touching, by use of force and facility, National Survey of Youth in Custody, 2012 58

Appendix table 6. Characteristics of juvenile facilities used to provide state-level estimates, National Survey of Youth in Custody, 2012 63

Appendix table 7. Percent of youth reporting sexual victimization, by type of incident and state, National Survey of Youth in Custody, 2012 64

List of figures

Figure 1. Confidence intervals at the 95%-level for juvenile facilities with the highest rates of sexual victimization, National Survey of Youth in Custody, 2012 13

Figure 2. Confidence intervals at the 95%-level for juvenile facilities with high rates of sexual victimization, by state, National Survey of Youth in Custody, 2012 18

Highlights

Prevalence of sexual victimization

- An estimated 9.5% of adjudicated youth in state juvenile facilities and state contract facilities (representing 1,720 youth nationwide) reported experiencing one or more incidents of sexual victimization by another youth or staff in the past 12 months or since admission, if less than 12 months.

- About 2.5% of youth (450 nationwide) reported an incident involving another youth, and 7.7% (1,390) reported an incident involving facility staff.

- An estimated 3.5% of youth reported having sex or other sexual contact with facility staff as a result of force or other forms of coercion, while 4.7% of youth reported sexual contact with staff without any force, threat, or explicit form of coercion.

- Among state juvenile facilities, the rate of sexual victimization declined from 12.6% in 2008-09 (when the first survey was conducted) to 9.9% in 2012. The decline in state facilities was linked to staff sexual misconduct with force (declining from 4.5% of youth in 2008-09 to 3.6% in 2012) and staff sexual misconduct without force (declining from 6.7% to 5.1%).

Facility rankings

- Thirteen facilities were identified as high-rate based on the prevalence of sexual victimization by youth or staff. Rates in each of these facilities had a 95%-confidence interval with a lower bound that was at least 35% higher than the average rate of sexual victimization among facilities nationwide.

- Two of the high-rate facilities—Paulding Regional Detention Center (Georgia) and Circleville Juvenile Correctional Facility (Ohio)—had sexual victimization rates of 30% or greater.

- Twenty-six facilities had no reported incidents of sexual victimization, and 14 were identified as low-rate after taking into account potential statistical variation. The upper bound of the 95%-confidence interval in these 14 facilities was less than half the average rate among all facilities listed in the survey.

- Youth held in state-owned or -operated facilities reported higher rates of staff sexual misconduct (8.2%) than those held in locally or privately operated facilities (4 5%).

State-level rates

- For the first time, state-level estimates were added to the survey to provide feedback to state administrators, especially those who operate facilities too small to provide facility-level estimates.

- Three states (Delaware, Massachusetts, and New York) and the District of Columbia had no reported incidents of sexual victimization.

- Four states (Georgia, Illinois, Ohio, and South Carolina) had high rates, based on the lower bound of the 95%-confidence interval of at least 35% higher than the national average. Each of these states had an overall sexual victimization rate exceeding 15%, which was primarily due to high rates of staff sexual misconduct.

Demographic and other youth characteristics

- Rates of reported sexual victimization varied among youth:

  - 8.2% of males and 2.8% of females reported sexual activity with staff.

  - 5.4% of females and 2.2% of males reported forced sexual activity with another youth at a facility.

  - White youth reported sexual victimization by another youth (4.0%) more often than black youth (1.4%) or Hispanic youth (2.1%).

  - Black youth reported a higher rate of sexual victimization by facility staff (9.6%) than white youth (6.4%) or Hispanic youth (6.4%).

  - Youth who identified their sexual orientation as gay, lesbian, bisexual, or other reported a substantially higher rate of youth-on-youth victimization (10.3%) than heterosexual youth (1.5%).

Circumstances surrounding the incident

- About 67.7% of youth victimized by another youth reported experiencing physical force or threat of force, 25.2% were offered favors or protection, and 18.1% were given drugs or alcohol to engage in sexual contact.

- Most youth-on-youth victims reported more than one incident (69.6%). An estimated 37.2% reported more than one perpetrator.

- Most youth victimized by another youth reported no physical injury (82.1%).

- Among the estimated 1,390 youth who reported victimization by staff, 89.1% were males reporting sexual activity with female staff and 3.0% were males reporting sexual activity with both male and female staff. In comparison, males comprised 91% of adjudicated youth in the survey and female staff accounted for 44% of staff in the sampled facilities.

- Most victims of staff sexual misconduct reported more than one incident (85.9%). Among these youth, nearly 1 in 5 (20.4%) reported 11 or more incidents.

- About 1 in 5 (20.3%) victims of staff sexual misconduct reported experiencing physical force or threat of force, 12.3% were offered protection, and 21.5% were given drugs or alcohol to engage in sexual contact.

- When youth were asked who initiated sexual contact, 36.4% reported that the facility staff always made the first move, 17.4% reported that they always made the first move, and 46.3% said that sometimes the facility staff made the first move and sometimes they did.

Sexual Victimization in Juvenile Facilities Reported by Youth, 2012

National Survey of Youth in Custody-2

Between February 2012 and September 2012, the Bureau of Justice Statistics completed the second National Survey of Youth in Custody (NSYC-2) in 273 state-owned or -operated juvenile facilities and 53 locally or privately operated facilities that held adjudicated youth under state contract. The survey was conducted by Westat (Rockville, MD), under a cooperative agreement with BJS. It was administered to 8,707 youth sampled from at least one facility in every state and the District of Columbia.

The NSYC-2 is part of the National Prison Rape Statistics Program, which collects reported sexual violence in administrative records and allegations of sexual victimization directly from victims through surveys of inmates in prisons and jails and surveys of youth held in juvenile correctional facilities. BJS has collected administrative records annually since 2004. Victim self-reports have been periodically collected since 2007 (adult facilities only), followed by surveys in 2008-09 (adult and juvenile facilities) and 2011-12 (adult and juvenile facilities).

The universe for the NSYC-2 was all adjudicated youth residing in facilities owned or operated by a state juvenile correctional authority and all state-placed adjudicated youth held under state contract in locally or privately operated juvenile facilities. The universe was restricted to facilities that housed youth for at least 90 days, contained more than 25% adjudicated youth, and housed at least 10 adjudicated youth.

> The Prison Rape Elimination Act of 2003 (P.L. 108-79; PREA) requires the Bureau of Justice Statistics (BJS) to carry out a comprehensive statistical review and analysis of the incidents and effects of prison rape for each calendar year. This report fulfills the requirement under Sec.4(c)(2)(B)(ii) of the act to provide a list of juvenile correctional facilities according to the prevalence of sexual victimization.

The NSYC-2 sampling frame included contract facilities in states where these facilities held at least 20% of all state-adjudicated youth or where fewer than 80 completed interviews were expected from youth held in state facilities. Since locally and privately operated facilities were more difficult to enroll and less likely to agree to participate in surveys related to the Prison Rape Elimination Act (PREA), the NSYC-2 excluded contract facilities in states in which they were not needed for state-level estimation. The NSYC-2 collected data from contract facilities in 15 states.

The NSYC-2 is a multistage probability sample providing representative data on state-adjudicated youth

Facilities were selected using a multistage stratified sample design based on information obtained from the Census of Juveniles in Residential Placement (CJRP), which was conducted in 2010 by the Office of Juvenile Justice and Delinquency Prevention. At the first stage, 446 facilities were selected from the 503 eligible facilities identified in the CJRP. All facilities with 20 or more state-placed adjudicated youth were included in the survey. Smaller facilities (housing between 10 and 19 adjudicated youth) were sampled with probabilities proportionate to their size. (See *Methodology* for sample description.)

Of the sampled facilities, 113 were later determined to be out-of-scope because they had closed, no longer held state-adjudicated youth, had merged with other facilities, or were no longer eligible for other reasons. Three additional sampled facilities were excluded due to scheduling problems and burden, and four facilities lacked consent for a sufficient number of youth to permit data collection. As a result, the NSYC-2 was conducted in 326 facilities, representing 18,138 state-adjudicated youth held nationwide in state-operated and locally or privately operated juvenile facilities in 50 states and the District of Columbia.

The NSYC-2 survey consisted of an audio computer-assisted self-interview (ACASI) in which youth used a touchscreen to interact with a computerized questionnaire and followed audio instructions delivered via headphones. The NSYC-2 used self-administered procedures to ensure the confidentiality of reporting youth and to encourage fuller reporting of victimization. The survey used audio technology to provide assistance to youth with varying levels of literacy and language skills. Approximately 99% of the interviews were conducted in English, and 1% in Spanish.

Administrators in each state, county, and private facility determined the type of consent required for youth to be eligible for participation. Youth who had reached the age of majority were able to self-consent, and contact with a parent or guardian was not required. Administrators provided *in loco parentis* (ILP) consent in 127 facilities for youth who were below the age of majority. *In loco parentis* is when administrators provide consent in the place of the parent to contact youth. Administrators required parental or guardian consent (PGC) from youth in 160 facilities and collected a mixture of ILP and PGC in 39 facilities, depending on the age of the sampled youth. Youth in all sampled facilities also had to assent to participate in the interview. (See *Methodology* for additional details on the consent process.)

In each sampled ILP facility, administrators were asked 5 weeks prior to data collection to provide a roster of all adjudicated youth assigned a bed. In other facilities (PGC or a mixture of consent requirements), administrators were asked to provide a roster 9 weeks prior to data collection. The initial rosters were updated to reflect youth admitted or discharged between the eighth and second week prior to data collection. Youth were randomly sampled from the initial and updated rosters.

Prior to the start of data collection, field staff assessed the interviewing capacity at each facility based on the number of available days, interviewing rooms, and interviewers. In facilities in which the NSYC-2 team had the capacity to complete all of the interviews, all youth for whom consent had been given, as well as youth who were able to self-consent, were selected. In other facilities, youth were randomly subsampled so the number of youth did not exceed interviewing capacity.

The result of this process yielded a sample of 22,944 state-adjudicated youth held nationwide in state-owned or -operated juvenile facilities or placed in locally or privately operated juvenile facilities. A total of 9,703 youth participated in the survey. Of these, 8,707 youth completed the survey on sexual victimization, and 996 completed the survey on drug and alcohol use and treatment.

The NSYC-2 collected allegations of sexual victimization. Since participation in the survey was anonymous and reports were confidential, the NSYC-2 did not permit any follow-up investigation or substantiation through review of official records. Some allegations in the NSYC-2 may be untrue. At the same time, some youth may remain silent about any sexual victimization experienced in the facility.

Terms and definitions

Sexual victimization—any forced sexual activity with another youth (nonconsensual sexual acts and other sexual contacts) and all sexual activity with facility staff.

Nonconsensual sexual acts—any forced sexual acts with another youth and all sexual acts with facility staff involving contact with the penis and the vagina or anus; contact between the mouth and the penis, vagina, or anus; penetration of the anal or vaginal opening of another person by a hand, finger, or other object; and rubbing of another person's penis or vagina by a hand.

Other sexual contacts only—includes kissing on the lips or another part of the body, looking at private body parts, being shown something sexual, such as pictures or a movie, and engaging in some other sexual act that did not involve touching.

Staff sexual misconduct—all sexual activity with facility staff, including contact with the penis and the vagina or anus; contact between the mouth and the penis, vagina, or anus; penetration of the anal or vaginal opening of another person by a hand, finger, or other object; rubbing

of another person's penis or vagina by a hand; kissing on the lips or another part of the body; looking at private body parts; being shown something sexual, such as pictures or a movie; and engaging in some other sexual act that did not involve touching.

Staff sexual misconduct excluding touching—sexual activity with facility staff involving contact with the penis and the vagina or anus; contact between the mouth and the penis, vagina, or anus; penetration of the anal or vaginal opening of another person by a hand, finger, or other object; and rubbing of another person's penis or vagina by a hand.

Forced sexual activity—includes sexual activity between youth and facility staff as a result of physical force or threat of physical force; force or pressure of some other type (e.g., threatening with harm, threatening to get the youth in trouble, pressuring the youth, or forcing or pressuring in some other way); and in return for money, favors, protection, or other special treatment.

To address concerns of false reporting by youth, reports of victimization were checked for consistency across survey items. Interviews that contained response patterns considered to be extreme or highly inconsistent were excluded from victimization rate calculations. (See text box below for details.) After deleting interviews due to extreme or inconsistent responses and interviews that were incomplete, the NSYC-2 sexual victimization survey and survey of alcohol and drug use and treatment were completed by 59% of all eligible sampled youth. (See *Methodology* for further details on sampling and survey participation.)

Interviews checked for extreme and inconsistent response patterns

As with any survey, the NSYC-2 is subject to measurement error. To reduce this error, the survey incorporated several design features, including the use of an audio-assisted questionnaire delivered via headphones to address low levels of literacy; the use of "hot words" highlighted in a different color, which youth could access if they were uncertain about the definition; range checks for selected questions to guard against unrealistic values; and logic checks that asked youth to verify their responses. To assist youth who were having difficulty with the interview, the computer flagged those who spent a long period in particular sections of the interview and prompted the youth to obtain assistance from an interviewer. While these measures and others helped reduce error, they did not prevent it from occurring.

Once the interviews were completed, individual response patterns were assessed to identify interviews having extreme or internally inconsistent responses. Three response patterns were considered extreme and indicative of an unreliable interview overall. These patterns were—

- The core survey was completed in less than 10 minutes. Based on internal testing, it was determined to be extremely difficult for a respondent to seriously complete the interview in less than 10 minutes.

- The reported number of sexual contacts with staff or forced sexual contacts with other youth exceeded 1.5 incidents per day for every day since admission to the facility.

- During the data collection visit, the facility received specific reports from youth that they had entered false responses to the survey.

Out of 8,845 completed interviews, 67 had at least one of the extreme response patterns. These interviews were excluded from the calculations of sexual victimization.

Thirty additional indicators were developed to assess whether a youth showed signs that he or she did not fully understand the survey items, did not consistently report the details of events, or provided inconsistent responses. One indicator was providing unrealistic dates or personal information, and another indicator was an affirmative response to a debriefing item that asked about difficulty understanding questions on sexual activity. Other indicators compared responses in one section of the survey with responses in other sections. (See appendix 3 for a full list of the indicators.)

The results of these 30 indicators were combined into a total number for each youth. About 90.4% of youth did not record any inconsistent responses, 7.0% reported one inconsistent response, 1.8% reported two, and 0.8% reported three or more. For estimating sexual victimization rates, an additional 71 interviews were excluded based on three or more indicators of inconsistent responses.

Deleting extreme or inconsistent responses from estimates lowers the overall victimization rate since many of the indicators rely on checking the consistency of reported sexual victimization. The estimate for the overall sexual victimization rate would have been 10.4% without deleting any interviews. The rate dropped to 9.5% after deleting 138 interviews that had at least one extreme response or three or more inconsistent responses. If interviews with two or more inconsistent responses were deleted, then the rate would have dropped to approximately 7.9%. If interviews with one or more had been deleted, the rate would have been approximately 5.0%. The cutoff at three or more inconsistent responses was selected in recognition that youth could legitimately report some inconsistent information without invalidating their entire interview.

Prevalence of sexual victimization

About 10% of youth in state-owned or -operated juvenile facilities and state contract facilities reported one or more incidents of sexual victimization

Among the 8,707 youth who participated in the 2012 survey, 833 reported experiencing one or more incidents of sexual victimization. Since the NSYC-2 is a sample survey, weights were applied for sampled facilities and youth within facilities to produce national-level and facility-level estimates. The estimated number of adjudicated youth who reported experiencing sexual violence totaled 1,720 (or 9.5% of the 18,138 estimated adjudicated youth held in state-owned or -operated or state contract facilities covered by the survey) (table 1).

About 2.5% of adjudicated youth (an estimated 450 nationwide) reported an incident involving another youth, and 7.7% (1,390) reported an incident involving facility staff. Some youth reported sexual victimization by both another youth and facility staff (0.7%) (not shown in table). Sexual acts or contacts between youth with no report of force or coercion were excluded from all measures of sexual victimization.

The NSYC-2 screened for specific sexual activities in which youth may have been involved during the past 12 months or since admission to the facility, if less than 12 months. Youth were asked to report which of these activities involved another youth and which involved staff at the facility. Additionally, youth were asked if any of these activities happened because they were forced, threatened with force, pressured in another way, or offered money, favors, special protection or other special treatment. (See appendices 1 and 2 for specific survey questions.) Reports of unwilling youth-on-youth sexual activity were classified as either nonconsensual acts or other sexual contacts only.

Approximately 1.7% of youth (300 nationwide) said they had nonconsensual sex with another youth, including giving or receiving sexual gratification, and oral, anal, or vaginal penetration. An estimated 0.6% (110) of adjudicated youth said they had experienced one or more other unwilling sexual contacts only with other youth, such as looking at private body parts, unwanted kissing on the lips or another part of the body, and other unwanted touching of specific body parts in a sexual way.

Reports of staff sexual misconduct with youth were classified separately depending on whether the misconduct involved any force, threat, pressure, or offers of special favors or protection. An estimated 3.5% of youth (630 nationwide) reported that they had sex or other sexual contact with facility staff as a result of force or other forms of coercion, and an estimated 4.7% (850) of youth said they had sexual contact with facility staff without any force, threat, or other explicit form of coercion.

TABLE 1

Youth reporting sexual victimization, by type of incident, National Survey of Youth in Custody, 2012

Type of incident	National estimate[a]		
	Number of victims	Percent of youth victimized	Standard error
U.S. total	1,720	9.5%	0.4%
Youth-on-youth[b]	450	2.5%	0.2%
Nonconsensual sexual acts[c]	300	1.7	0.2
Other sexual contacts only[d]	110	0.6	0.1
Staff sexual misconduct	1,390	7.7%	0.4%
Force reported[e]	630	3.5	0.2
Excluding touching[c]	550	3.1	0.2
Other sexual contacts only[d]	40	0.2	0.1
No report of force	850	4.7	0.3
Excluding touching[c]	770	4.3	0.3
Other sexual contacts only[d]	70	0.4	0.1

Note: Detail may not sum to total because youth may have reported multiple victimizations or due to item nonresponse. Youth were asked to report on any victimization involving another youth or facility staff in the past 12 months or since admission to the facility, if less than 12 months.

[a]Based on reports from 8,707 adjudicated youth interviewed in 326 juvenile facilities and weighted to represent the number of adjudicated youth held in the nation. (See *Methodology*.)

[b]Excludes acts in which there was no report of force.

[c]Includes contact between the penis and the vagina or the penis and the anus; contact between the mouth and the penis, vagina, or anus; penetration of the anal or vaginal opening of another person by a hand, finger, or other object; and rubbing of another person's penis or vagina by a hand.

[d]Includes kissing on the lips or another part of the body; looking at private body parts; showing something sexual, such as pictures or a movie; and engaging in some other sexual contact that did not involve touching.

[e]Includes physical force, threat of force, other force or pressure, and other forms of coercion, such as being given money, favors, protections, or special treatment.

Source: Bureau of Justice Statistics, National Survey of Youth in Custody, 2012.

Rates of sexual victimization in state juvenile facilities decreased from 12.6% in 2008-09 to 9.9% in 2012

Rates of sexual victimization reported by youth in state-owned or -operated juvenile facilities declined from an estimated 12.6% in 2008-09 to 9.9% in 2012 (table 2). These estimates were based on interviews of 8,156 adjudicated youth in 169 sampled facilities in the NSYC-1 and 7,356 youth in 272 sampled facilities in the NSYC-2. To compare rates across the two surveys, youth held in locally or privately operated facilities were excluded in both surveys due to differences in sampling and coverage. The criteria used to define inconsistent, extreme, and incomplete responses were also made comparable between the NSYC-1 and NSYC-2.

The overall decrease in reported sexual victimization was due to statistically significant declines in staff sexual misconduct with force (declining from 4.5% in the NSYC-1 to 3.6% in the NSYC-2) and staff sexual misconduct without force (from 6.7% to 5.1%). Although youth reported slightly lower rates of youth-on-youth sexual victimization in 2012 than in 2008-09 (decreasing from 2.8% to 2.5%), the decline was not statistically significant.

Declines in sexual victimization rates were linked to fewer youth held in large facilities, a drop in average exposure time, and rising positive views of facility staff and fairness

While many factors may account for the decline in sexual victimization rates in state juvenile facilities, the NSYC-2 identified four important trends linked to sexual victimization rates.

TABLE 2

Youth reporting sexual victimization in state juvenile facilities, by type of incident and survey year, National Survey of Youth in Custody, 2008–09 and 2012

Type of incident	Percent of youth reporting any sexual victimization in state-owned or -operated facilities only[a]		Standard error	
	NSYC-1 2008–09*	NSYC-2 2012	NSYC-1 2008–09	NSYC-2 2012
U.S. total	12.6%	9.9%**	0.5%	0.5%
Youth-on-youth[b]	2.8%	2.5%	0.3%	0.3%
Nonconsensual sexual acts[c]	2.1	1.7	0.2	0.2
Other sexual contacts only[d]	0.5	0.6	0.2	0.1
Staff sexual misconduct	10.7%	8.2%**	0.4%	0.4%
Force reported[e]	4.5	3.6**	0.3	0.3
Excluding touching[c]	4.1	3.2**	0.3	0.3
Other sexual contacts only[d]	0.4	0.2	0.1	0.1
No report of force	6.7	5.1**	0.3	0.3
Excluding touching[c]	6.1	4.6**	0.3	0.3
Other sexual contacts only[d]	0.5	0.5	0.1	0.1

Note: Detail may not sum to total because youth may have reported multiple victimizations or due to item nonresponse. Youth were asked to report on any victimization involving another youth or facility staff in the past 12 months or since admission to the facility, if less than 12 months.

*Comparison group.

**Difference with comparison group is significant at the 95%-confidence level.

[a]Based on reports from 8,156 adjudicated youth in 169 facilities interviewed in NSYC-1 and 7,356 youth in 272 facilities interviewed in NSYC-2 and weighted to represent the number of adjudicated youth held in comparable state-owned or -operated juvenile facilites. Excludes youth held in locally or privately operated facilities. (See Methodology.)

[b]Excludes acts in which there was no report of force.

[c]Includes contact between the penis and the vagina or the penis and the anus; contact between the mouth and the penis, vagina, or anus; penetration of the anal or vaginal opening of another person by a hand, finger, or other object; and rubbing of another person's penis or vagina by a hand.

[d]Includes kissing on the lips or another part of the body; looking at private body parts; showing something sexual, such as pictures or a movie; and engaging in some other sexual contact that did not involve touching.

[e]Includes physical force, threat of force, other force or pressure, and other forms of coercion, such as being given money, favors, protections, or special treatment.

Source: Bureau of Justice Statistics, National Survey of Youth in Custody, 2012.

The proportion of youth held in large facilities dropped sharply from 2008-09 to 2012:

- An estimated 65.6% of youth in the NSYC-1 were held in large facilities (with 101 or more adjudicated youth), compared to 53.2% of youth in the NSYC-2 (table 3).

- The proportion of youth held in medium facilities (with 51 to 100 youth) increased from 17.0% in 2008-09 to 24.0% in 2012.

- In each survey, sexual victimization rates were two to three times higher in large facilities than facilities with 10 to 25 youth.

Among sampled youth, the average time youth had been held in facilities declined:

- As measured by the average exposure time (i.e., 12 months or the elapsed time between the admission date and the survey date for youth admitted to the facility in the last 12 months), the time that youth were at risk of sexual victimization decreased. The percentage of youth who were in the facility for less than 5 months increased from 20.9% in the NSYC-1 to 26.9% in NSYC-2.

- When combined with a decline in the rates of sexual victimization reported by youth held for 5 to 6 months (from 13.4% to 10.0%) and youth held for 7 to 12 months (from 14.4% to 11.6%), this decline in exposure time was linked to the decrease in the overall rate of sexual victimization.

Youth in the NSYC-2 reported more positive opinions about the facility and fairness in how the facilities were run than youth in the NSYC-1. (See *Methodology* for a list of survey items.) Based on eight separate items, youth who had no positive opinions of the facility also reported the highest rates of sexual victimization (a third of sampled youth in each survey). Youth with four or more positive opinions about the facility had the lowest sexual victimization rates (5.5% in the NSYC-1 and 3.9% in NSYC-2).

TABLE 3
Percent of youth reporting sexual victimization, by youth opinions about facility and staff, facility size, and exposure time, National Survey of Youth in Custody, 2008–09 and 2012

| | Percent of all youth | | Youth reporting any sexual victimization | | | |
| | | | Percent | | Standard error | |
	NSYC-1 2008–09*	NSYC-2 2012	NSYC-1 2008–09*	NSYC-2 2012	NSYC-1 2008–09*	NSYC-2 2012
Number of positive opinions about the facility and fairness of facility policies[a]						
None	7.1%	6.4%	32.6%	33.8%	2.5%	2.6%
1–3	41.9	38.3**	17.7	14.7**	0.8	0.9
4–8	51.0	55.4**	5.5	3.9**	0.5	0.4
Number of positive opinions about the facility staff[b]						
None	19.2%	17.1%**	22.9%	23.5%	1.4%	1.4%
1–3	26.0	22.9**	15.9	13.9	0.8	1.3
4–8	54.8	60.0**	7.4	4.6**	0.6	0.4
Number of adjudicated youth in facility[c]						
10–25	6.0%	8.0%	6.7%	4.2%	3.2%	1.0%
26–50	11.4	14.1	12.7	6.3**	2.7	0.8
51–100	17.0	24.0**	10.3	9.3	1.8	0.8
101 or more	65.6	53.2**	13.7	12.2	0.4	0.7
Average exposure time in facility[d]						
Less than 5 months	20.9%	26.9%**	7.4%	7.6%	1.1%	0.6%
5–6 months	38.2	34.3	13.4	10.0**	0.8	0.7
7–12 months	40.9	38.8	14.4	11.6**	0.7	0.8

Note: Estimates based on reports from adjudicated youth in comparable facilities in both surveys. Excludes youth held in locally or privately operated facilities.

*Comparison group.

**Difference with comparison group is significant at the 95%-confidence level.

[a]Based on 8 questions about what happens at the facility and perceptions of fairness. (See *Methodology* for list of items.)

[b]Based on 8 questions about facility staff related to their conduct and how they treat youth at the facility. (See *Methodology* for list of items.)

[c]Among facilities in the NSYC-2, 0.7% had fewer than 10 adjudicated youth. This row is not shown since there is no comparison group in NSYC-1.

[d]Based on the length of time between the admission date and the survey date. Exposure was capped at 12 months. If the admission date was more than 12 months prior to the survey, youth were asked only about their experiences in the last 12 months.

Source: Bureau of Justice Statistics, National Survey of Youth in Custody, 2012.

Youth in the NSYC-2 also expressed more positive opinions of the facility staff than youth in the NSYC-1. When asked if staff were "good role models," "friendly," "genuinely car[ing]," "helpful," "fun to be with," "disrespectful," "hard to get along with," or "mean," an estimated 60.0% responded with positive views in the NSYC-2 (up from 54.8% in NSYC-1). Across both surveys, youth with four or more positive opinions had the lowest sexual victimization rates (7.4% in the NSYC-1 and 4.6% in NSYC-2), while youth with no positive opinions of the facility staff had the highest sexual victimization rates (22.9% in the NSYC-1 and 23.5% in NSYC-2).

While changing youth opinions may reflect improved conditions in the facilities between the NSYC-1 and NSYC-2 surveys, they may also be the result of lower levels of sexual victimization by staff. Although the exact cause or effect is unknown, the improved perceptions of the facility and facility staff are associated with the decline in the percentage of staff sexual misconduct which underlie the overall decline in sexual victimization.

Facility-level rates

After taking into account statistical variation, thirteen facilities were identified as high-rate

Of the 157 juvenile facilities eligible for comparison in the NSYC-2, 13 had an overall victimization rate that was identified as high rate (table 4). Though other measures may be considered when comparing facilities, the overall victimization rate is a measure of prevalence that includes all reports of unwilling sexual activity between youth and all reports of staff sexual misconduct, regardless of the level of coercion and type of sexual activity.[1]

An exact ranking for all facilities as required under the PREA cannot be statistically produced. As with any survey, the NSYC-2 estimates are subject to sampling error because they are based on a sample of youth rather than a complete enumeration. In some facilities, youth were subsampled; in other facilities, all youth were selected. In 155 of the listed

[1]Facility-level rates were based on the reports of adjudicated youth who were in the facility at least 2 weeks prior to the time of the interview. Excludes the experiences of non-adjudicated youth and youth held in the facility in the past 12 months who were not in the facility when the interviews were conducted.

TABLE 4
Juvenile facilities with the highest rates of sexual victimization, National Survey of Youth in Custody, 2012

Facility name	Number of respondents[b]	Response rate[c]	Youth reporting any sexual victimization[a]		
				95%-confidence interval	
			Percent	Lower bound	Upper bound
All facilities - U.S. total	8,667	60.1%	9.5%	8.7%	10.3%
Paulding Reg. Yth. Det. Ctr. (GA)	28	56.9	32.1	21.7	44.7
Circleville Juv. Corr. Fac. (OH)	66	77.6	30.3	24.4	36.9
Birchwood (SC)	24	83.3	29.2	20.6	39.5
Eastman Yth. Dev. Campus (GA)	116	82.9	24.4	20.7	28.5
Scioto Juv. Corr. Fac. (OH)[d]	69	69.0	23.2	18.1	29.2
Arkansas Juv. Assess. & Trtmt. Ctr. (AR)[d]	69	84.3	23.2	17.7	29.7
Corsicana Res. Trtmt. Ctr. (TX)	76	71.0	22.4	17.1	28.7
Boys State Training School (IA)[e]	69	80.2	21.7	17.1	27.2
Illinois Yth. Ctr. Joliet (IL)	114	75.7	21.1	16.6	26.3
Augusta Yth. Dev. Campus (GA)	51	82.3	20.9	15.8	27.1
Sumter Yth. Dev. Campus (GA)	86	67.4	20.8	15.7	27.0
John G. Richards (SC)[f]	40	76.9	20.0	14.1	27.6
Cuyahoga Hills Juv. Corr. Fac. (OH)	89	68.5	19.8	14.6	26.2

Note: High-rate facilities are those in which the lower bound of the confidence interval is larger than 1.35 times the national average. Facilities housed males only unless otherwise noted.
[a]Weighted percentage of youth reporting one or more incidents of sexual victimization involving another youth or facility staff in the past 12 months or since admission to the facility, if less than 12 months.
[b]Number of adjudicated youth who participated in the sexual victimization component of the survey. Excludes 40 youth due to item nonresponse.
[c]Response rate accounts for different probabilities of selection among youth and the exclusion of interviews with extreme or inconsistent responses. (See *Methodology* for details.)
[d]Facility housed both males and females. Both were sampled at this facility.
[e]See *Methodology* for discussion of extreme and inconsistent responses and handling of false responses.
[f]Would not be included among high-rate facilities if additional exclusion criteria for extreme and inconsistent responses were used. (See *Methodology* for details.)
Source: Bureau of Justice Statistics, National Survey of Youth in Custody, 2012.

facilities (see appendix table 1), some of the eligible youth did not participate in the survey due to the absence of consent by a parent or guardian, self-consent, or assent by the selected youth.

To address nonresponse bias, adjustments were applied to the base weights. To address sampling variability, a 95%-confidence interval was provided for each survey estimate. Typically, multiplying the standard error by 1.96 and then adding or subtracting the result from the estimate produces the confidence interval. This interval expresses the range of values that could result among 95% of the different samples.

For small samples and estimates close to 0% or 100%, as is the case with the NSYC-2, using the standard error to construct the 95%-confidence interval may not be reliable. An alternative developed by E.B. Wilson has performed better than the traditional method when constructing a confidence interval.[2,3] When applied to large samples, the traditional and the Wilson confidence intervals are virtually identical.

Consequently, the tables in this report containing facility-level and state-level estimates provide confidence intervals based on Wilson's methodology (tables 4 through 8, table 10, table 17, appendix tables 2 through 5, and appendix table 7). Tables

containing national estimates are based on traditional standard error calculations (tables 1 through 3, table 9, and tables 11 through 16). (See *Methodology* for details.)

The 13 facilities were identified as having high rates because the lower bound of the 95%-confidence interval was at least 35% higher than the average rate among all facilities (9.5%) (figure 1).[4] Although the NSYC-2 cannot uniquely identify the facility with the highest victimization rate, two facilities had rates of 30% or greater. Paulding Regional Detention Center (Georgia) recorded an overall rate of 32.1%, and Circleville Juvenile Correctional Facility (Ohio) recorded a rate of 30.3%. Birchwood (South Carolina) had a victimization rate of 29.2%.

While each of the 13 facilities had high rates, some facilities not classified as having high rates were not statistically different from the 13 high-rate facilities due to sampling error.

[2]Brown, L.D., Cai, T., & DasGupta, A. (2001). "Interval Estimation for a Binomial Proportion." *Statistical Science*, 16(2), 101-117.

[3]Wilson, E.B. (1927). "Probable Inference, the Law of Succession, and Statistical Inference." *Journal of the American Statistical Association*, 22(158), pp. 209-212.

[4]The criterion of at least 35% higher than the average rate was established to identify a small group of facilities that would be considered as having high rates. Other criteria reflecting variation in the estimates would have identified a smaller or larger number of facilities.

FIGURE 1

Confidence intervals at the 95%-level for juvenile facilities with the highest rates of sexual victimization, National Survey of Youth in Custody, 2012

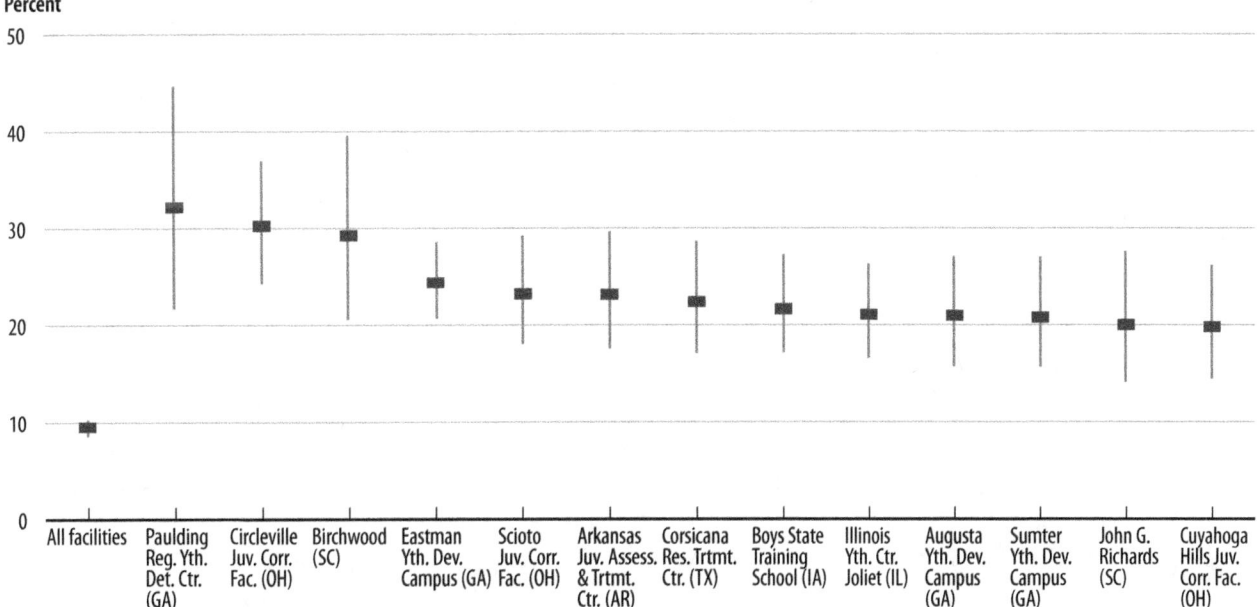

Source: Bureau of Justice Statistics, National Survey of Youth in Custody, 2012.

26 facilities had no reported sexual victimizations, and 14 of these facilities were identified as low rate

The NSYC-2 is unable to provide an exact identification of the facilities with the lowest rates of sexual victimization. Twenty-six of the sampled juvenile facilities (17%) had no reported incidents of sexual victimization (see appendix table 2). Rates in each of the 26 facilities are subject to sampling error, depending on which youth were selected and the number of surveys completed by youth within the facility. Although in each facility the lower bound of the confidence interval was 0%, the upper bound varied depending on the number of completed interviews.

Among the 157 surveyed facilities, 14 were identified as low-rate facilities for sexual victimization based on the percentages of youth who reported incidents and the upper bounds of the 95%-confidence intervals that were less than half the average rate among all facilities (table 5). All of the 14 low-rate facilities had no reported incidents of sexual victimization with the upper bound confidence interval between 1.5% and 4.7%. Ft. Bellefontaine Campus (Missouri), Owensboro Treatment Center (Kentucky), and Grand Mesa Youth Services Center (Colorado) had no reported incidents and had confidence intervals with upper bounds below 2%.

TABLE 5
Juvenile facilities with the lowest rates of sexual victimization, National Survey of Youth in Custody, 2012

| | | | Youth reporting any sexual victimization[a] | | |
| | | | | 95%-confidence interval | |
Facility name	Number of respondents[b]	Response rate[c]	Percent	Lower bound	Upper bound
All facilities - U.S. total	8,667	60.1%	9.5%	8.7%	10.3%
Ft. Bellefontaine Campus (MO)	23	100	0.0	0.0	1.5
Owensboro Trtmt. Ctr. (KY)	22	100	0.0	0.0	1.6
Grand Mesa Yth. Srvcs. Ctr. (CO)[d]	33	94.3	0.0	0.0	1.9
Waverly Reg. Yth. Ctr. (MO)	34	91.9	0.0	0.0	2.0
Cadet Leadership & Education Program (KY)	18	100	0.0	0.0	2.4
Green River Yth. Dev. Ctr. (KY)	18	100	0.0	0.0	2.4
Rich Hill Yth. Dev. Ctr. (MO)	17	100	0.0	0.0	3.0
Mt. View Yth. Srvcs. Ctr. (CO)[d]	42	75.0	0.0	0.0	3.1
RiverBend Yth. Transition Fac. (OR)	32	80.0	0.0	0.0	3.4
Camp Florence Yth. Transition Fac. (OR)	19	90.5	0.0	0.0	3.8
Camino Nuevo Yth. Ctr. (CNYC) (NM)[d]	44	69.8	0.0	0.0	3.9
McFadden Ranch (TX)	29	78.4	0.0	0.0	4.0
Sierra-Osage Trtmt. Ctr. (MO)[d]	17	89.5	0.0	0.0	4.6
Girardot Ctr. for Yth. and Families (MO)	16	94.1	0.0	0.0	4.7

Note: Low-rate facilities are those in which the upper bound of the confidence interval is lower than 0.5 times the national average. Facilities housed males only unless otherwise noted.

[a]Weighted percentage of youth reporting one or more incidents of sexual victimization involving another youth or facility staff in the past 12 months or since admission to the facility, if less than 12 months.

[b]Number of adjudicated youth who participated in the sexual victimization component of the survey. Excludes 40 youth due to item nonresponse.

[c]Response rate accounts for different probabilities of selection among youth and the exclusion of interviews with extreme or inconsistent responses. (See *Methodology*.)

[d]Facility housed both males and females. Both were sampled at this facility.

Source: Bureau of Justice Statistics, National Survey of Youth in Custody, 2012.

Youth held in high-rate facilities reported high rates of nonconsensual sexual activity

Among the 13 high-rate facilities, most reports of sexual victimization involved nonconsensual sexual acts with another youth and sexual acts with facility staff excluding touching (table 6). When rates of sexual victimization were limited to the most serious nonconsensual acts (excluding touching only, kissing on the lips or another body part, and engaging in other less serious acts), the percentages of youth reporting one or more incidents remained high (between 16.2% and 28.8%).

Circleville Juvenile Correctional Facility (Ohio) had a 28.8% rate of sexual victimization excluding touching and a confidence interval with a lower bound (22.9%) that was more than three times the national average (7.1%). Six other facilities had rates of sexual victimization excluding touching that were more than double the national average and a confidence interval with a lower bound that was more than twice the national average.

TABLE 6

Juvenile facilities with the highest rates of sexual victimization, by type of contact, National Survey of Youth in Custody, 2012

Facility name	Youth reporting nonconsensual sexual acts excluding touching[a]			Youth reporting other sexual contacts only[b]		
		95%-confidence interval			95%-confidence interval	
	Percent	Lower bound	Upper bound	Percent	Lower bound	Upper bound
All facilities - U.S. total	7.8%	7.1%	8.6%	1.0%	0.8%	1.3%
Circleville Juv. Corr. Fac. (OH)	28.8	22.9	35.5	1.5	0.5	4.3
Paulding Reg. Yth. Det. Ctr. (GA)	25.9	15.7	39.8	3.7	1.0	13.1
Birchwood (SC)	22.7	14.6	33.6	0.0	0.0	4.2
Eastman Yth. Dev. Campus (GA)	21.3	17.6	25.6	1.7	0.8	3.4
Corsicana Res. Trtmt. Ctr. (TX)	19.7	14.6	26.1	2.6	1.2	5.9
Illinois Yth. Ctr. Joliet (IL)	19.5	15.4	24.3	0.9	0.3	3.0
Boys' State Training School (IA)	18.8	14.4	24.3	2.9	1.4	5.9
Cuyahoga Hills Juv. Corr. Fac. (OH)	18.8	13.9	24.9	0.9	0.2	3.5
Sumter Yth. Dev. Campus (GA)	18.5	13.6	24.7	2.3	1.0	5.3
Scioto Juv. Corr. Fac. (OH)[c]	17.9	13.4	23.5	3.0	1.3	6.9
John G. Richards (SC)	17.5	12.0	24.8	0.0	0.0	2.9
Augusta Yth. Dev. Campus (GA)	17.3	12.5	23.5	1.9	0.7	4.9
Arkansas Juv. Assess. & Trtmt. Ctr. (AR)[c]	16.2	12.1	21.4	4.3	2.5	7.4

Note: High-rate facilities are those in which the lower bound of the confidence interval is larger than 1.35 times the national average. Facilities housed males only unless otherwise noted.

[a]Includes contact between the penis and the vagina or the penis and the anus; contact between the mouth and the penis, vagina, or anus; penetration of the anal or vaginal opening of another person by a hand, finger, or other object; and rubbing of another person's penis or vagina by a hand. Includes any of these acts with a staff member and any forced acts with another youth.

[b]Includes kissing on the lips or other part of the body; looking at private body parts; showing something sexual, such as pictures or a movie; and engaging in some other sexual act that did not involve touching.

[c]Facility housed both males and females. Both were sampled at this facility.

Source: Bureau of Justice Statistics, National Survey of Youth in Custody, 2012.

Of the 13 high-rate facilities, one facility (Arkansas Juvenile Assessment and Treatment Center) had a youth-on-youth sexual victimization rate that exceeded 10% (table 7). In two facilities, none of the interviewed youth reported any sexual victimization by other youth in the facility. However, one of these facilities, Paulding Regional Youth Detention Center (Georgia), had the highest rate of staff-on-youth sexual victimization (31.0%).

High percentages of youth reported staff sexual misconduct in which no force, threat, or other forms of coercion were involved. Seven of the 13 high-rate facilities had rates of staff sexual misconduct (with no report of force) that were more than twice the national average (table 8). Two facilities—Paulding Regional Youth Detention Center and Circleville Juvenile Correctional Center—had a confidence interval around the rate of staff sexual misconduct (with no force) with a lower bound that exceeded 10%.

TABLE 7
Juvenile facilities with the highest rates of sexual victimization, by type of incident, National Survey of Youth in Custody, 2012

| | Youth-on-youth[a] | | | Staff sexual misconduct[b] | | |
| | | 95%-confidence interval | | | 95%-confidence interval | |
Facility name	Percent	Lower bound	Upper bound	Percent	Lower bound	Upper bound
All facilities - U.S. total	2.5%	2.1%	3.0%	7.7%	7.0%	8.4%
Arkansas Juv. Assess. & Trtmt. Ctr. (AR)[c]	11.6	8.1	16.4	14.2	10.4	19.2
Corsicana Res. Trtmt. Ctr. (TX)	7.9	5.0	12.2	18.4	13.4	24.8
Scioto Juv. Corr. Fac. (OH)[c]	5.8	3.2	10.1	18.8	14.0	24.9
John G. Richards (SC)	5.0	2.3	10.4	15.0	9.9	22.0
Birchwood (SC)	4.0	1.4	10.6	29.2	20.6	39.5
Cuyahoga Hills Juv. Corr. Fac. (OH)	3.8	1.9	7.3	16.0	11.0	22.7
Circleville Juv. Corr. Fac. (OH)	3.0	1.4	6.4	28.8	22.9	35.5
Eldora State Training School for Boys (IA)	2.9	1.4	6.0	18.8	14.4	24.2
Sumter Yth. Dev. Campus (GA)	2.3	1.0	5.3	18.3	13.5	24.3
Illinois Yth. Ctr. Joliet (IL)	1.8	0.7	4.2	20.0	15.6	25.2
Eastman Yth. Dev. Campus (GA)	0.8	0.3	2.2	23.5	19.8	27.7
Paulding Reg. Yth. Det. Ctr. (GA)	0.0	0.0	6.4	31.0	20.9	43.4
Augusta Yth. Dev. Campus (GA)	0.0	0.0	2.0	20.9	15.8	27.1

Note: High-rate facilities are those in which the lower bound of the confidence interval is larger than 1.35 times the national average. Facilities housed males only unless otherwise noted.

[a]Weighted percentage of youth reporting one or more incidents of sexual victimization involving another youth in the past 12 months or since admission to the facility, if less than 12 months.

[b]Weighted percentage of youth reporting one or more incidents of sexual victimization involving facility staff in the past 12 months or since admission to the facility, if less than 12 months.

[c]Facility housed both males and females. Both were sampled at this facility.

Source: Bureau of Justice Statistics, National Survey of Youth in Custody, 2012.

TABLE 8
Juvenile facilities with the highest rates of staff sexual victimization, by use of force, National Survey of Youth in Custody, 2012

| | Youth reporting staff sexual misconduct with force[a] | | | Youth reporting staff sexual misconduct with no report of force | | |
| | | 95%-confidence interval | | | 95%-confidence interval | |
Facility name	Percent	Lower bound	Upper bound	Percent	Lower bound	Upper bound
All facilities - U.S. total	3.5%	3.0%	4.0%	4.7%	4.1%	5.3%
Birchwood (SC)	21.7	14.2	31.8	4.5	1.6	12.1
Circleville Juv. Corr. Fac. (OH)	15.2	10.6	21.1	18.2	13.4	24.2
Illinois Yth. Ctr. Joliet (IL)	14.0	10.1	19.2	6.2	3.9	9.6
Augusta Yth. Dev. Campus (GA)	13.6	9.5	19.3	9.3	6.0	14.0
Eastman Yth. Dev. Campus (GA)	13.1	10.2	16.8	12.3	9.5	15.8
Scioto Juv. Corr. Fac. (OH)[b]	13.0	8.9	18.7	6.0	3.3	10.6
Corsicana Res. Trtmt. Ctr. (TX)	10.5	6.8	16.0	10.7	7.2	15.6
Sumter Yth. Dev. Campus (GA)	10.3	7.0	15.0	9.2	6.0	13.8
Paulding Reg. Yth. Det. Ctr. (GA)	7.1	2.7	17.6	25.9	16.1	39.0
Eldora State Training School for Boys (IA)	5.8	3.5	9.5	13.0	9.5	17.6
John G. Richards (SC)	5.0	2.3	10.4	10.0	6.0	16.3
Arkansas Juv. Assess. & Trtmt. Ctr. (AR)[b]	4.0	2.3	6.8	8.9	6.1	12.8
Cuyahoga Hills Juv. Corr. Fac. (OH)	2.6	1.0	6.7	13.4	9.1	19.2

Note: High-rate facilities are those in which the lower bound of the confidence interval is larger than 1.35 times the national average. Facilities housed males only unless otherwise noted.

[a]Includes physical force, threat of force, other force or pressure, and other forms of coercion, such as being given money, favors, protections, or special treatment.

[b]Facility housed both males and females. Both were sampled at this facility.

Source: Bureau of Justice Statistics, National Survey of Youth in Custody, 2012.

Rates of sexual victimization were strongly associated with basic facility characteristics

An initial examination of available facility characteristics revealed significant differences in sexual victimization rates:[5]

■ State adjudicated youth held in state-owned or -operated facilities reported higher rates of staff sexual misconduct (8.2%) than those held in locally or privately operated facilities (4.5%) (table 9).

[5]For the first time, the NSYC-2 included a facility questionnaire to obtain in-depth information about each sampled facility. Items included data on facility staff by sex, occupation, and length of service; staff turnover; personnel screening; facility capacity, occupancy, and crowding; use and type of video surveillance by area covered; type of facility and primary function; types of youth held and special problems; and types of treatment programs. These data and other facility characteristics will be examined in a second report from the NSYC-2.

■ Female-only facilities had the highest rates of youth-on-youth sexual victimization (5.7%), while male-only facilities had the highest rates of staff sexual misconduct (8.2%).

■ Small facilities (those holding 25 or fewer adjudicated youth) had the lowest rates of staff sexual misconduct (1.3% among facilities with 1 to 9 youth, and 2.9% among facilities with 10 to 25 youth). Larger facilities had higher rates of staff sexual misconduct (5.4% for those with 26 to 50 youth, 6.8% with 51 to 100 youth, and 10.2% with more than 100 youth).

■ Facilities in which youth were held for an average of less than 5 months had the lowest rates of sexual victimization (6.8%), compared to facilities in which youth were held for longer periods (10.0% in facilities with an average exposure time of 5 to 6 months, and 11.3% in facilities with an average of 7 to 12 months).

TABLE 9

Prevalence of sexual victimization, by type of incident and selected facility characteristics, National Survey of Youth in Custody, 2012

Facility characteristic	Number of youth[a]	Percent of youth reporting any sexual victimization by—			Standard error		
		Both youth and staff	Another youth	Facility staff	Both youth and staff	Another youth	Facility staff
Operating agency							
State*	15,500	9.9%	2.4%	8.2%	0.5%	0.3%	0.4%
Non-state[b]	2,600	6.9**	2.9	4.5**	1.0	0.5	0.9
Sex of youth housed							
Males only*	13,600	9.7%	2.0%	8.2%	0.5%	0.2%	0.4%
Females only	800	6.7**	5.7**	2.2**	1.3	1.2	0.7
Both males and females	3,700	9.4	3.7**	7.2	0.9	0.7	0.8
Number of adjudicated youth[c]							
1–9	300	2.5%	1.2%	1.3%	1.1%	0.7%	0.8%
10–25*	2,000	4.5	2.2	2.9	0.9	0.5	0.7
26–50	2,800	7.6**	2.6	5.4**	0.9	0.6	0.7
51–100	4,300	8.4**	2.3	6.8**	0.7	0.4	0.6
101 or more	8,700	12.0**	2.7	10.2**	0.7	0.4	0.6
Average exposure time in facility[d]							
Less than 5 months*	5,500	6.8%	1.5%	5.6%	0.5%	0.2%	0.5%
5–6 months	6,200	10.0**	2.4**	8.3**	0.6	0.3	0.6
7–12 months	6,400	11.3**	3.5**	8.8**	0.9	0.6	0.7

*Comparison group.

**Difference with comparison group is significant at the 95%-confidence level.

Note: Weighted percentage of youth reporting one or more incidents of sexual victimization involving another youth or facility staff in the past 12 months or since admission to the facility, if less than 12 months.

[a]Estimated number of adjudicated youth in facilities covered by the NSYC-2 rounded to nearest 100.

[b]Refers to locally and privately operated juvenile facilities in 15 states where a significant number of state-adjudicated youth were held in these facilities. The rates do not reflect local and contract facilities that hold state-adjudicated youth in other states. (See *Methodology*.)

[c]Based on the number of adjudicated youth assigned beds in the facility. The number of youth reported at the time of enrollment (approximately 2 months prior to the visit), was used for six facilities unable to provide these data in the facility questionnaire.

[d]The average exposure period for youth in the facility was based on reports from all interviewed youth. Exposure time was based on the number of months each youth in the sexual victimization survey was in the facility during the 12 months prior to the survey or since admission, if less than 12 months. (See *Methodology*.)

Source: Bureau of Justice Statistics, National Survey of Youth in Custody, 2012.

State-level rates

In addition to facility-level and national-level estimates, the NSYC-2 was designed to provide state-level estimates. State estimates were added to provide more comprehensive feedback to administrators, especially to those who operate facilities that were too small to provide reliable facility-level estimates. State-level rates are particularly valuable in states comprised of small facilities. At least half of facilities in the NSYC-2 (169 of 326 sampled facilities) were determined to be too small (with fewer than 15 completed interviews) or fell below standards of statistical precision needed for publishing facility-level survey rates. These facilities held approximately 30% of adjudicated youth covered in the NSYC-2. (See *Methodology* for discussion of reporting criteria.)

Using each facility's measure of size, the state-level rates were created by combining the weighted average of the facility-level rates for published facilities with an estimate for the unpublished facilities. Except for 11 states, all published and unpublished facility rates were used (table 10). Including the unpublished facility with the rates for the published facilities would have made it possible to derive the rate for each unpublished facility. Excluding the 11 facilities in these states had a minimal impact on the state estimates. These facilities represented 10% or less of adjudicated youth for all but 2 of the 11 states: Delaware and Nebraska. (See *Methodology* for discussion of state-level estimation.)

Three states (Delaware, Massachusetts, and New York) and the District of Columbia had no reported incidents of sexual victimization.[6] Although the samples of participating youth were relatively small, the upper bound of the 95%-confidence interval in the District of Columbia and each of the three states fell below the national average (9.5%) across all states.

Four states were identified as high-rate for sexual victimization

While the NSYC-2 should not be used to provide an exact ranking of states, the same criteria that were used to classify facilities may be used to classify states. Six states had rates of sexual victimization that exceeded 15% (figure 2). Four of these states (Georgia, Illinois, Ohio, and South Carolina) may be identified as having high rates since the lower bound of the confidence interval around each estimate was at least 35% higher than the average rate among all facilities (9.5%).

A high percentage of adjudicated youth reported staff sexual misconduct in these four states (not shown; see appendix table 7). An estimated 17.1% of adjudicated youth in Ohio, 17.0% in South Carolina, 15.0% in Georgia, and 13.7% in Illinois reported one or more incidents of staff sexual misconduct. The lower bound of the confidence interval was 35% higher than the national average (7.7%) for estimates in each of these states. None of these states had rates of youth-on-youth sexual victimization that met the criteria to be classified as high.

---

[6]Although none of the 51 youth interviewed in New York reported an incident of sexual victimization, the response rate was extremely low (12.5%). The state required youth to give permission to contact his or her guardian before NSYC-2 survey staff could request consent from the guardian and subsequent assent from the youth. This resulted in low participation among sampled youth.

FIGURE 2

Confidence intervals at the 95%-level for juvenile facilities with high rates of sexual victimization, by state, National Survey of Youth in Custody, 2012

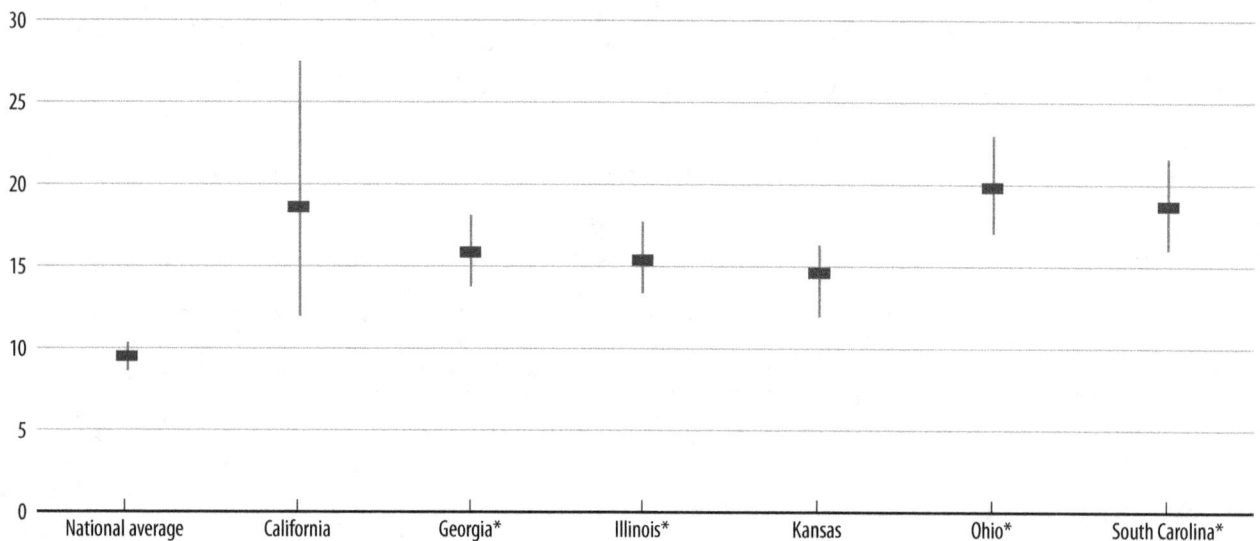

*High-rate states with the lower bound around the confidence interval that was at least 35% higher than the national average.

Source: Bureau of Justice Statistics, National Survey of Youth in Custody, 2012.

TABLE 10

Percent of youth reporting sexual victimization, by state, National Survey of Youth in Custody, 2012

State	Number of respondents	Weighted percent[a]	Percent of youth reporting any sexual victimization	
			95%-confidence interval	
			Lower bound	Upper bound
U.S. total[b]	8,667	9.5%	8.7%	10.3%
Alabama	132	13.2	10.1	17.1
Alaska	101	3.4	2.1	5.6
Arizona	149	9.0	6.1	13.3
Arkansas	230	13.7	11.5	16.2
California	167	18.6	12.0	27.5
Colorado	424	8.7	7.1	10.6
Delaware	21	0.0	0.0	8.4
District of Columbia	24	0.0	0.0	8.5
Florida	573	5.2	3.6	7.6
Georgia	497	15.8	13.8	18.1
Hawaii	37	10.8	6.3	17.9
Idaho	184	3.8	2.8	5.1
Illinois	451	15.4	13.3	17.7
Indiana	370	10.4	8.8	12.2
Iowa	214	7.9	4.2	14.4
Kansas	252	14.6	12.0	17.8
Kentucky	222	3.9	2.9	5.3
Louisiana	226	5.2	3.2	8.4
Maine	90	5.0	3.0	8.4
Maryland	51	4.8	1.2	17.0
Massachusetts	87	0.0	0.0	2.2
Michigan	60	10.5	5.4	19.5
Minnesota	61	3.4	1.1	10.2
Mississippi	42	11.9	7.9	17.6
Missouri	517	4.0	3.4	4.7
Montana	23	13.0	5.4	28.4
Nebraska	24	4.2	0.9	17.7
Nevada	75	10.3	5.6	18.3
New Jersey	174	6.3	3.3	11.5
New Mexico	95	2.5	0.8	7.1
New York	51	0.0	0.0	9.0
North Carolina	105	4.2	2.1	8.3
North Dakota	54	7.3	4.4	11.9
Ohio	329	19.8	17.0	23.0
Oklahoma	46	18.4	8.4	35.5
Oregon	561	10.5	9.4	11.7
Pennsylvania	139	7.5	4.2	13.1
Rhode Island	39	5.1	1.9	12.8
South Carolina	108	18.7	16.1	21.5
South Dakota	45	5.4	1.5	18.3
Tennessee	134	13.0	8.5	19.5
Texas	633	11.6	9.7	13.8
Utah	100	10.3	6.3	16.4
Vermont	15	6.7	3.1	13.7
Virginia	174	11.3	7.3	17.0
Washington	160	5.7	3.1	10.0
West Virginia	109	13.5	11.5	15.9
Wisconsin	148	6.5	4.2	9.9
Wyoming	56	1.9	0.5	6.9

Note: Data for Connecticut and New Hampshire are not reported due to insufficient data to provide a state rate. (See *Methodology* for estimation of state-level rates.)

[a]Based on weighted percentage of youth reporting one or more incidents of sexual victimization involving another youth or facility staff in the past 12 months or since admission to the facility, if less than 12 months.

[b]Includes data from respondents in all facilities that participated in the NSYC-2. Excludes 40 youth who did not report enough information to determine their victimization by youth and staff.

Source: Bureau of Justice Statistics, National Survey of Youth in Custody, 2012.

Demographic and other youth characteristics

Rates of sexual victimization were strongly related to specific youth characteristics

Rates of sexual victimization varied among youth:

- Males reported sexual activity with facility staff more often than females. An estimated 8.2% of males, compared to 2.8% of females, reported experiencing one or more incidents of sexual activity with staff (table 11).

- Females reported forced sexual activity with other youth more often than males. About 5.4% of females and 2.2% of males reported forced sexual activity with another youth at the facility.

- Rates of staff sexual misconduct were higher among youth age 17 (8.0%) and those age 18 or older (8.7%) than youth age 15 or younger (5.8%).

- White youth (4.0%) reported sexual victimization by another youth more often than black (1.4%) and Hispanic (2.1%) youth.

TABLE 11
Prevalence of sexual victimization, by type of incident and selected youth victim characteristics, National Survey of Youth in Custody, 2012

Victim characteristic	Number of youth[a]	Percent of youth reporting any sexual victimization by—			Standard error		
		Both youth and staff	Another youth	Facility staff	Both youth and staff	Another youth	Facility staff
Sex							
Male*	16,500	9.7%	2.2%	8.2%	0.5%	0.2%	0.4%
Female	1,600	6.9**	5.4**	2.8**	0.8	0.8	0.6
Age							
15 or younger*	3,000	7.6%	2.5%	5.8%	0.7%	0.4%	0.7%
16	4,000	8.8	2.2	7.3	0.9	0.6	0.9
17	5,200	9.7	2.4	8.0**	0.9	0.5	0.7
18 or older	6,000	10.7**	2.8	8.7**	0.6	0.3	0.6
Race/Hispanic origin							
White*,b	6,500	9.7%	4.0%	6.4%	0.7%	0.5%	0.5%
Black[b]	7,700	10.3	1.4**	9.6**	0.6	0.3	0.6
Hispanic	3,000	7.5	2.1**	6.4	1.0	0.4	0.9
Other[b,c]	600	6.9	2.8	4.6	1.3	0.8	1.2
Two or more races[b]	400	8.9	2.2	6.7	1.7	1.0	1.6
Sexual orientation							
Heterosexual*	15,900	8.9%	1.5%	7.8%	0.5%	0.2%	0.4%
Non-heterosexual[d]	2,200	14.3**	10.3**	7.5	1.3	1.2	1.2
Any prior sexual assault							
Yes	2,500	17.4%**	9.6%**	9.7%**	1.6%	1.3%	1.1%
No*	15,600	8.2	1.3	7.3	0.4	0.2	0.4
Sexually assaulted at another facility							
Yes	300	52.3%**	33.5%**	29.3%**	4.9%	5.2%	4.6%
No*	17,900	8.6	1.8	7.3	0.4	0.1	0.4
Time in facility							
Less than 1 month	1,000	7.1%	1.9%	5.9%	1.0%	0.6%	1.0%
1–5 months*	8,800	8.0	1.9	6.3	0.6	0.3	0.5
6–11 months	4,700	10.6**	2.5	8.7**	0.8	0.5	0.7
12 months or more	3,600	12.4**	4.2**	10.1**	1.0	0.6	0.9

*Comparison group.

**Difference with comparison group is significant at the 95%-confidence level.

Note: Weighted percentage of youth reporting one or more incidents of sexual victimization involving another youth or facility staff in the past 12 months or since admission to the facility, if less than 12 months.

[a]Estimated number of adjudicated youth covered by the NSYC-2 rounded to nearest 100.

[b]Excludes persons of Hispanic or Latino origin.

[c]Includes American Indian, Alaska Native, Asian, Native Hawaiian, and other Pacific Islander.

[d]Includes gay, lesbian, bisexual, and other sexual orientations.

Source: Bureau of Justice Statistics, National Survey of Youth in Custody, 2012.

- Black youth reported a higher rate of sexual victimization by facility staff (9.6%) than white (6.4%) and Hispanic (6.4%) youth.

- Youth with a non-heterosexual sexual orientation reported a substantially higher rate of youth-on-youth victimization (10.3%) than heterosexual youth (1.5%).

- Rates of staff-on-youth sexual victimization increased with the length of time a youth was held in the facility. An estimated 10.1% of youth who were in the facility for a year or longer reported sexual activity with a staff member, compared to 5.9% of youth who were in the facility less than 1 month, 6.3% of youth who were in the facility between 1 and 5 months, and 8.7% of youth who were held between 6 and 11 months.

- Youth who experienced any prior sexual assault were more than twice as likely to report experiencing one or more sexual assaults in the current facility (17.4%) than those with no sexual assault history (8.2%).

- Among youth who were previously sexually assaulted at another correctional facility, over half (52.3%) reported being sexually victimized at the current facility within the last 12 months or since admission, if less than 12 months. Among these youth, an estimated 33.5% were sexually victimized by another youth at the current facility, and 29.3% were victimized by staff.

Circumstances surrounding the incident

Most youth-on-youth victims (69.6%) reported more than one incident, and 37.2% reported more than one perpetrator

In the NSYC-2, victims were also asked to provide information about the circumstances surrounding their victimization, including the number of times it happened, characteristics of the perpetrators, the type of physical force or pressure, when and where the incidents occurred, and whether or not they reported injury.

Data provided by youth who reported sexual victimization by another youth revealed that—

- About 69.6% were victimized more than once, while 18.9% were victimized more than 10 times (table 12).

- An estimated 37.2% of youth-on-youth victims were victimized by more than one perpetrator.

TABLE 12

Experiences of youth-on-youth victims of sexual victimization, National Survey of Youth in Custody, 2012

Experience	Victims of any sexual victimization by another youth	
	Percent	Standard error
Number of incidents		
1	30.4%	6.1%
2	11.9	3.1
3–5	24.5	4.2
6–10	14.3	4.5
11 or more	18.9	3.3
Victimized by more than one perpetrator		
Yes	37.2%	5.0%
No	62.8	5.0
Race of perpetrator[a]		
White	65.1%	4.7%
Black	57.2	5.1
Other[b]	27.5	5.1
Hispanic or Latino origin of perpetrator		
Yes	40.6%	5.6%
No	59.4	5.6
Any of the perpetrators in a gang		
Yes	52.4%	5.5%
No	47.6	5.5

Note: Based on an estimated 450 youth sexually victimized by another youth.

[a]Detail sums to more than 100% because some youth reported more than one victimization or more than one perpetrator.

[b]Includes American Indian, Alaska Native, Asian, Native Hawaiian, and other Pacific Islander.

Source: Bureau of Justice Statistics, National Survey of Youth in Custody, 2012.

- An estimated 65.1% of victims said that they were victimized by a youth who was white, 57.2% said they were victimized by a youth who was black. In comparison, 32.2% of all adjudicated youth held in sampled facilities were white and 45.9% were black.

- The majority of victims (52.4%) said they were victimized at least once by a youth known to be in a gang.

- About 67.7% of victims reported experiencing physical force or threat of force, 25.2% were offered favors or protection, and 18.1% were given drugs or alcohol to engage in the sexual act or other sexual contact (table 13).

- Most youth victimized by another youth (82.1%) reported no physical injury.

Youth-on-youth sexual victimization occurred in areas throughout the facilities

Among youth who reported unwanted sexual activity with another youth, 44.4% said they were victimized at least once in their room or sleeping area, and 31.0% said they were victimized at least once in the room or sleeping area of another youth. Nearly a third (32.7%) reported at least one incident taking place in a shower or bathroom, 25.0% said they were victimized in a recreation area, and 59.1% said at least one incident happened in some other common area, such as a classroom, library, kitchen, office, closet, or supply room.

Youth-on-youth sexual victimization was more common in the evening (between 6 p.m. and midnight) than at any other time. An estimated 60.9% of the youth who reported unwanted sexual activity with another youth said at least one of the incidents occurred during those hours.

TABLE 13

Circumstances surrounding youth-on-youth sexual victimization, National Survey of Youth in Custody, 2012

Circumstance	Victims of any sexual victimization by another youth	
	Percent	Standard error
Type of pressure or force[a]		
Force/threat of force	67.7%	4.7%
Gave victim drugs/alcohol	18.1	3.4
Offered favors or protection	25.2	3.7
Type not reported	24.2	4.9
Victim injured		
Yes	17.9%	3.5%
No	82.1	3.5
Where occurred[a]		
In victim's room/sleeping area	44.4%	5.2%
In room/sleeping area of another youth	31.0	5.6
Shower/bathroom[b]	32.7	3.9
Recreation area[b]	25.0	5.2
Other common area[b,c]	59.1	5.8
Off facility grounds	5.3	1.5
Time of day[a]		
6 a.m. to noon	29.3%	4.4%
Noon to 6 p.m.	43.5	5.1
6 p.m. to midnight	60.9	4.7
Midnight to 6 a.m.	20.3	3.4

Note: Weighted percentage of youth reporting one or more incidents of sexual victimization involving another youth in the past 12 months or since admission to the facility, if less than 12 months.

[a]Detail sums to more than 100% because some youth reported more than one victimization or more than one location.

[b]Based on all victims who reported a location of occurrence.

[c]Includes a classroom, library, workshop, kitchen or other workplace, office, someone else's room or sleeping area, closet, or supply room.

Source: Bureau of Justice Statistics, National Survey of Youth in Custody, 2012.

Most perpetrators of staff sexual misconduct were female

An estimated 92.4% of all youth who reported staff sexual misconduct said they were victimized by female facility staff (table 14).[7] Among the estimated 1,390 adjudicated youth who reported victimization, 89.1% were males reporting sexual activity with female staff only, and 3.0% were males reporting sexual activity with both female and male staff.

---

[7]An estimated 91% of all adjudicated youth held in the sampled facilities were male. Approximately 44% of all staff and 34% of frontline staff in participating facilities were female.

An estimated 630 youth reported physical force, threat of force, and other forms of pressure and coercion by facility staff. Among these victims, 20.5% reported a male staff member as the perpetrator (15.0% involved male staff only and 5.5% involved both male and female staff).

Male staff members represented a smaller percentage of perpetrators among youth reporting staff sexual misconduct that did not involve any force. Among the 840 youth who experienced staff sexual misconduct without force, 5.1% reported the involvement of a male staff member (2.7% involved male staff only and 2.4% involved both male and female staff).

TABLE 14
Victims of staff sexual misconduct, by use of force and sex of youth and staff, National Survey of Youth in Custody, 2012

	Percent of youth reporting any sexual victimization			Standard error		
	All victims	Force reported*	No report of force	All victims	Force reported	No report of force
All victims	100%	100%	100%	:	:	:
Male victim						
Male staff	5.2%	9.9%	2.0%**	1.5%	3.1%	0.8%
Female staff	89.1	79.3	94.6**	1.8	3.4	1.4
Both male and female staff	3.0	5.5	2.4	0.7	1.5	0.8
Female victim						
Male staff	2.4%	5.1%	0.7%**	0.7	1.5	0.6
Female staff	0.2	0.2	0.4	0.2	0.2	0.3
Both male and female staff	0.1	--	--	0.1	--	--
Estimated number of victims[a]	1,390	630	840	:	:	:

Note: In facilities covered by the NSYC-2, an estimated 91% of adjudicated youth were male. Based on staff counts provided by 321 facilities responding to the facility survey, 44% of staff members were female.

*Comparison group.

**Difference with comparison group is significant at the 95%-confidence level.

: Not calculated.

--Less than 0.05%.

[a]Detail sums to more than total because some youth reported more than one victimization.

Source: Bureau of Justice Statistics, National Survey of Youth in Custody, 2012.

Most victims of staff sexual misconduct (85.9%) reported more than one incident, while 20.4% reported being victimized more than 10 times

Data provided by youth who were sexually victimized by facility staff revealed that—

- Approximately a third (32.0%) of youth were victimized by more than one staff member (table 15).

- About 20.3% of youth experiencing physical force or threat of force, 12.3% were offered favors or protection, and 21.5% were given drugs or alcohol to engage in the sexual act or other sexual contact.

- Most youth victimized by staff (93.9%) were not physically injured.

- Approximately 80.9% of victims said at least one incident occurred in a common area, such as a classroom, library, kitchen, office, closet, or supply room. Nearly half (48.9%) of victims said at least one incident occurred in a shower or bathroom, and more than half (52.5%) said they were victimized by staff in the youth's room or sleeping area.

- Staff sexual misconduct most commonly occurred between 6 p.m. and midnight (53.5%), followed by incidents occurring between noon and 6 p.m. (49.4%).

- An estimated 41.1% of staff sexual misconduct victims said that the first sexual activity occurred during the first month at the facility (10.6% within the first 24 hours, 6.9% during the remainder of the first week, and 23.6% during the remainder of the month).

TABLE 15
Circumstances surrounding incidents of staff sexual misconduct, National Survey of Youth in Custody, 2012

Circumstance	Victims of any staff sexual misconduct	
	Percent	Standard error
Number of incidents		
1	14.2%	1.5%
2	18.3	1.8
3–5	32.2	2.3
6–10	15.0	1.9
11 or more	20.4	1.6
Victimized by more than one staff member		
Yes	32.0%	2.3%
No	68.0	2.3
Type of pressure or force[a]		
Force/threat of force	20.3%	2.1%
Gave victim drugs/alcohol	21.5	1.8
Offered favors or protection	12.3	1.6
None[b]	63.4	2.6
Victim injured		
Yes	6.1%	1.4%
No	93.9	1.4
Where occurred[a,c]		
In victim's room/sleeping area	52.5%	2.7%
Shower/bathroom	48.9	2.5
Recreation area	14.4	1.8
Other common area[d]	80.9	1.7
Off of facility grounds	9.7	1.4
Time of day[a]		
6 a.m. to noon	42.9%	2.5%
Noon to 6 p.m.	49.4	2.4
6 p.m. to midnight	53.5	2.5
Midnight to 6 a.m.	40.2	2.2
When incident first happened[e]		
During first 24 hours	10.6%	1.5%
During first week	6.9	1.1
During first month	23.6	2.5
During first 2 months	11.6	1.6
After first 2 months	40.0	2.7
Not reported	7.3	1.1

Note: Based on an estimated 1,390 youth reporting one or more incidents of staff sexual misconduct in the past 12 months or since admission to the facility, if less than 12 months.

[a]Detail sums to more than 100% because some youth reported more than one victimization or more than one location.

[b]Includes type of force or pressure not reported.

[c]Based on all victims who reported a location occurrence.

[d]Includes a classroom, library, workshop, kitchen or other workplace, office, someone else's room or sleeping area, closet, and supply room.

[e]Based on when the youth first came to the facility on the current admission.

Source: Bureau of Justice Statistics, National Survey of Youth in Custody, 2012.

Staff sexual misconduct was linked to other inappropriate contact with youth

As a result of the high rate of staff sexual misconduct reported in the NSYC-1 (10.3%), new items were added to the NSYC-2 questionnaire to better understand the circumstances surrounding incidents. Youth were asked a series of questions related to their relationship with the facility staff prior to sexual contact (table 16). Among victims of staff sexual misconduct—

- Nearly two-thirds said that staff told them about their personal life outside of work (69.1%), treated them like a favorite or better than other youth (63.6%), or gave them a special gift that the staff would not have given to most other youth (62.3%).

- Almost half (49.2%) said the staff member gave them pictures or wrote them letters. Nearly a third (29.8%) said that the staff member contacted them in other ways when the staff member was not at the facility.

- More than a third (36.7%) said youth gave the staff member pictures of themselves, and more than a quarter (28.1%) said youth gave the staff member a special gift.

When youth were asked who initiated the sexual contact, 36.4% said that the facility staff always made the first move, 17.4% reported that the youth always made the first move, and 46.3% said that sometimes the facility staff made the first move and sometimes the youth did.

Youth were also asked to describe the sexual relationship with staff. Nearly half (46.3%) said the incident was usually just sexual. An estimated 40.1% said the sexual contact was more like friends with benefits, and 13.6% said that they really cared about each other.

TABLE 16
Victims of staff sexual misconduct, by relationship characteristic, National Survey of Youth in Custody, 2012

Relationship characteristic	Victims of any staff sexual misconduct	
	Percent	Standard error
Prior contact/relationship between youth and staff		
Staff told youth about personal life outside of work	69.1%	2.1%
Staff gave youth pictures or wrote letters	49.2	2.5
Staff gave youth special gift	62.3	2.3
Staff treated youth as special/favorite	63.6	2.4
Youth gave staff pictures or wrote letters	36.7	2.5
Youth gave staff special gift	28.1	2.2
Staff member contacted youth in other ways when staff not at the facility	29.8	2.1
Who initiated the sexual contact*		
Always the facility staff	36.4%	2.3%
Always the youth	17.4	1.9
Sometimes the youth and sometimes staff	46.3	2.4
Youth's perception of the relationship		
Really cared about each other	13.6%	1.7%
Friends with benefits	40.1	2.7
Usually just sexual	46.3	2.8

Note: Based on an estimated 1,390 youth reporting one or more incidents of staff sexual misconduct in the past 12 months or since admission to the facility, if less than 12 months.

*Includes youth who reported one or more incidents.

Source: Bureau of Justice Statistics, National Survey of Youth in Custody, 2012.

Methodology

The second National Survey of Youth in Custody (NSYC-2) was conducted in all 50 states and the District of Columbia by Westat (Rockville, MD), under a cooperative agreement with the Bureau of Justice Statistics (BJS). Data collection was conducted in 326 juvenile facilities between February and September 2012.

Interviewing juveniles in residential facilities on such sensitive topics required extensive preparations with agency and facility administrators prior to the interview. These preparations ranged from methods to obtain consent, procedures to file mandatory reports of child abuse or neglect, arrangements for counseling in case a youth became upset, and logistical support to physically carry out the interviewing. The specific procedures that had to be negotiated with state and local authorities were—

- Consent to interview minors—22 states and the District of Columbia provided consent *in loco parentis* (ILP), in which the state agency acting as the guardian provided consent; 20 states required written consent and 3 states required either verbal or written parental or guardian consent (PGC); and 5 states allowed for a combination of ILP and PGC.

- Mandatory reporting of abuse or neglect—all survey staff in direct contact with youth had to comply with state and local reporting requirements when a youth made a verbal statement suggesting abuse or neglect. Jurisdictions provided contact information and instructions for submitting reports to an agency outside of the facility (e.g., local Child Protective Services).

- Counseling services—jurisdictions were asked to identify both facility-based and external resources for counseling services in the event a youth would become emotionally upset during the interview or make a specific request to the interviewer for such services.

The NSYC-2 comprised two questionnaires—a survey of sexual victimization and a survey of past drug and alcohol use and treatment. Youth were randomly assigned one of the questionnaires so that, at the time of the interview, the content of the survey remained unknown to facility staff and the survey interviewers.

The interviews, which averaged approximately 30 minutes in length, used audio computer-assisted self-interviewing (ACASI) data collection methods. Youth interacted with the computer-administered questionnaires using a touchscreen and synchronized audio instructions delivered through headphones. Youth could choose to take the interview in either English or Spanish. Youth completed the interview in private, with the interviewer remaining in the room but in a position that did not offer a view of the computer screen.

A total of 9,703 youth participated in the NSYC-2. Of these, 8,707 youth completed the survey on sexual victimization and passed editing and consistency checks. A total of 996 completed the survey on drug and alcohol use and treatment.

Sampling of facilities

The universe for the survey was all adjudicated youth residing in facilities owned or operated by a state juvenile correctional authority and all state-adjudicated youth held under contract in locally or privately operated juvenile facilities. The universe was restricted to facilities that housed youth for at least 90 days, held at least 25% adjudicated youth, and held at least 10 adjudicated youth at the time of the survey. These restrictions were imposed to allow sufficient time to obtain consent from the parent or guardian.

The NSYC-2 sampling frame included contract facilities in states where contract facilities held at least 20% of all state-adjudicated youth or where fewer than 80 completed interviews were expected from youth held in state facilities. Since locally and privately operated facilities were more difficult to enroll and less likely to participate in surveys related to the Prison Rape Elimination Act (PREA), the NSYC-2 excluded contract facilities in states not needed for state-level estimation. Given these parameters, the NSYC-2 collected data from contract facilities in 15 states.

A multistage stratified sample design was used. At the first stage of selection, 446 facilities were selected from 503 eligible facilities in the United States. Facilities were selected using the 2010 Census of Juveniles in Residential Placement (CJRP), conducted by the Office of Juvenile Justice and Delinquency Prevention.

- All facilities in the frame with 20 or more adjudicated youth were sampled with certainty. This threshold yielded at least one sample facility in each state except Vermont, which had one state facility that housed fewer than 10 adjudicated youth. (This facility was selected to meet the PREA mandate of including at least one facility in every state.)

- Facilities with 10 to 19 adjudicated youth were sampled with probability proportional to size. For state facilities, the measure of size was the number of adjudicated youth reported in the 2010 CJRP. For the contract facilities, it was the number of state-adjudicated placed youth. The selection probability of these facilities was their measure of size divided by 20. This number corresponded to the measure of size for the smallest certainty facility.

- A supplemental sample was taken to include additional contract facilities that were misclassified during the initial sample selection. An additional 10 facilities were selected from among 24 reclassified facilities.

Subsequent state-level and facility-level enrollment efforts determined 113 of these 446 facilities to be out-of-scope. Facilities were out-of-scope under any of the following conditions:

- closed or were schedule to close prior to data collection (35)
- did not house youth for more than 90 days (49)
- did not house state-placed youth (13) or adjudicated youth (6)
- merged with another enrolled facility (6) or was split into two separate facilities (1)
- housed only youth with a limited cognitive capacity who were unable to self-consent or assent or complete the survey (2)
- no longer a juvenile corrections facility (1).

Of the remaining 333 eligible juvenile facilities, 4 lacked consent for a sufficient number of youth to permit data collection, and 3 were not visited due to issues related to scheduling and burden.

Selection of youth

Rosters of adjudicated youth were provided by facilities granting *in loco parentis* (ILP) consent 5 weeks prior to data collection. Facilities granting other forms of consent (either PGC or some combination of PGC and ILP) provided a roster 9 weeks prior to data collection. Rosters were updated weekly, up to 2 weeks prior to the collection, to reflect youth who were subsequently admitted to or discharged from each facility.

Interviewing capacity at each facility was assessed based on the number of available days, interviewing rooms, and interviewers. In facilities determined to have sufficient capacity, all eligible youth were selected for the survey. In other facilities, youth were randomly subsampled so the number of youth did not exceed interviewing capacity.

A total of 22,944 youth were initially selected. Among these individuals, 5,402 left prior to the interview team arriving at the facility and 940 were excluded based on subsampling within the facility. Once the discharges and excluded cases were removed from the pool of selected youth, 16,602 youth remained eligible for the NSYC-2.

Approximately 26% of youth did not participate because consent from the parent or guardian could not be obtained, 8% refused to complete the interview, and 6% were nonrespondents for other reasons (e.g., they did not complete the entire interview, they were not at the facility at the time of visit, the facility denied access, or they were excluded due to extreme or inconsistent response patterns).

Weighting and nonresponse adjustments for facility and national estimates

To generate facility estimates, each youth was assigned an initial weight that corresponded to the inverse of the probability of selection within each facility. A series of adjustments was applied to the initial weight to compensate for nonresponse. These adjustments were completed in three steps:

1. Adjustment cells were constructed based on each youth's most serious offense, race or Hispanic origin, age, sex, and the number of days held in the facility.

2. An adjustment required a minimum nonresponse cell size of 10 responding youth. In many facilities, this resulted in no nonresponse adjustment, as either the facility had too few interviews (fewer than 20) to create multiple cells or the differences between respondents and nonrespondents were not significant. In facilities where significant differences were observed, 2 to 4 nonresponse cells were created.

3. After an initial nonresponse adjustment, the weights within a facility were examined and trimmed to reduce undue influence from a small number of respondents with very large weights. If the highest weight was 4 times greater than the lowest weight in the facility, the highest weights were trimmed and the difference in weighted counts was distributed to the remaining youth. After trimming, the high-to-low ratio in the final weight would equal to 4.

To generate national estimates, each sampled facility was assigned a weight that corresponded to the inverse of the facility's probability of selection into the sample, and the weight was adjusted for facility nonresponse. The adjusted facility weights were then multiplied by the youth weights that resulted from the three-step process outlined above, thereby producing a national-level youth weight.

Calculating response rates

A total of 8,845 youth completed the survey on sexual victimization, and 996 completed the survey on drug and alcohol use and treatment. After excluding 138 youth whose interviews were deleted due to extreme or inconsistent responses in the sexual victimization survey, the NSYC-2 achieved a weighted overall response rate of 59% for all sampled youth. (See box on page 9 for discussion of extreme and inconsistent response patterns.)

Separate response rates were calculated for each participating facility. (See appendix table 1.) Within each facility, a base weight was created for each youth in the sexual victimization survey by taking the inverse of each youth's probability of selection. In most facilities, youth selection probabilities were the same; however, in facilities in which youth were subsampled or where rosters contained duplicate records, selection probabilities varied.

An initial facility response rate was calculated by summing the base weights for all youth who completed the sexual victimization survey and dividing it by the sum of the base weights for all sampled youth. Ineligible youth in each facility were excluded.

A final response rate was calculated to account for deleted interviews that contained extreme or inconsistent responses. (See discussion on page 9.) This was achieved by multiplying the initial facility response rate by an adjustment ratio. In each facility, this ratio represented the sum of final weights for all interviewed youth (excluding those with extreme or inconsistent responses) divided by the sum of final weights for all interviewed youth (including those with extreme or inconsistent responses). This final adjusted response rate was then multiplied by 100.

Calculations for Adobe Mountain School (Arizona) illustrate the measurement of these weighted facility-level response rates. This facility listed 284 youth on its roster. Among those listed, 124 were subsampled out, and no interview was attempted with them. Among the remaining 160 sampled youth, 144 were sampled for the sexual victimization survey and 16 for the survey of past drug and alcohol use and treatment. Of the 144 eligible youth, 105 completed the NSYC-2 sexual victimization survey (72.9%). After adjusting for the probability of selection for each youth, the 105 youth who completed the sexual victimization survey represented the 284 youth in this facility. Five of the interviewed youth (4.8%) provided extreme or three or more inconsistent responses and were excluded. After adjusting for these cases, the resulting facility response rate was 69.4% (0.729 times 0.952 times 100).

Selecting facilities for publication

Facility-level estimates were published only if they met a set of criteria to ensure that the estimates had minimum reliability. The estimates were required to meet all of the following criteria: (1) they were based on at least 15 youth who completed the sexual victimization survey, (2) they represented facilities with a 30% response rate or greater, and (3) they had a minimum coefficient of variation of 30% and were significantly precise to detect a high victimization rate (i.e., if they had a hypothetical victimization rate of 25% or greater, the lower bound of the confidence interval would be 35% higher than the national rate). (See *Standard errors and confidence intervals section* below for discussion of sampling precision.)

Based on these criteria, facility-level estimates were reported for 157 (of the 326) participating facilities. (See appendix tables 2, 3, 4, and 5 for facility estimates by type of sexual victimization.) These facilities accounted for approximately 70% of the adjudicated youth covered in NSYC-2.

State-level estimates

State-level estimates were generated using a weighted average of the facility-level rates. Except for 11 states in which one participating facility did not meet the criteria for publication, all published and unpublished state rates were used. In these 11 states, publishing a rate for the entire state, along with the rates for the published facilities, would have made it possible to derive the rate for the unpublished facility.

Four approaches were used to produce state estimates:

1. In 14 states and the District of Columbia, facility-level estimates were published for all participating facilities. A state-level rate was calculated by dividing the combined weighted counts of youth reporting sexual victimization in all facilities by the combined weighted count of all youth in all of the participating facilities. (These states included Arizona, Hawaii, Idaho, Indiana, Maine, Mississippi, Nevada, Ohio, Oregon, Rhode Island, Vermont, West Virginia, Wisconsin, and Wyoming.)

2. In 11 states, facility-level estimates were published for all participating facilities except one. A state-level rate was calculated by dividing the combined weighted counts of youth reporting sexual victimization in the published facilities by the combined weighted counts of all youth in the published facilities. (These states included Alabama, Colorado, Delaware, Illinois, Kansas, Montana, Nebraska, New Mexico, South Carolina,

Tennesee, and Virginia. The excluded facility accounted for 10% or less of the state population in all states except Delaware and Nebraska.)

3. In 17 states, one or more facilities had a published rate, and two or more facilities did not have a published rate. A state-level rate was estimated by calculating a weighted average from the unpublished facilities and combining it with the weighted average of the estimates from published facilities. (These states included Alaska, Arkansas, Florida, Georgia, Iowa, Kentucky, Louisiana, Michigan, Minnesota, Missouri, New Jersey, North Carolina, North Dakota, Pennsylvania, Texas, Utah, and Washington.)

4. In six states, no facility-level estimates were published, but all facilities together met the publication criteria. A state-level rate was estimated by combining the data from all unpublished facilities based on the original probabilities of selection and weighting adjustments. (These states included California, Massachusetts, Maryland, New York, Oklahoma, and South Dakota.)

In two states (Connecticut and New Hampshire), no facility-level estimates were published and all facilities combined did not meet the publication criteria. In these states, the NSYC-2 could not provide a state-level estimate.

Standard errors and confidence intervals

Survey estimates are subject to sampling error because they are based on a sample rather than a complete enumeration. Within each facility, the sampling error varies by the size of the estimate, the number of completed interviews, and the size of the facility. Due to the relatively small samples within many of the selected facilities, it is especially important to consider the possibility of sampling error when interpreting the survey results.

Estimates of the standard errors for selected measures of sexual victimization are presented in tables that provide national-level estimates. These estimates may be used to construct confidence intervals around the survey estimates (e.g., numbers, percentages, and rates), as well as to test for significant differences between the estimates.

For example, the 95%-confidence interval around the percentage of male youth who reported sexual victimization by another youth is approximately 2.2% plus or minus 1.96 times 0.2% (or 1.8% to 2.6%). Based on similarly conducted samples, 95% of the intervals would be expected to contain the true (but unknown) percentage.

The standard errors may also be used to construct confidence intervals around differences in the estimates. The 95%-confidence interval comparing the percentage of male youth (2.2%) and female youth (5.4%) who reported sexual victimization by another youth may be calculated. The confidence interval around the difference of 3.2% is approximately plus or minus 1.96 times 0.82% (the square root of the standard error of the difference). The standard error of the difference is calculated by taking the square root of the sum of each standard error squared (e.g., the square root of $(0.2)^2$ plus $(0.8)^2$). Since the interval (1.6% to 4.8%) does not include zero, the difference between male youth and female youth in the rate of sexual victimization by other youth is considered statistically significant.

To express the possible variation due to sampling associated with facility-level estimates, tables in this report provide lower and upper bounds of the related 95%-confidence intervals. Since many facility samples are small and the estimates are close to zero, confidence intervals were constructed using an alternative method developed by E.B. Wilson. Computationally, this method produces an asymmetrical confidence interval around the facility estimates, in which the lower bound is constrained to be greater than or equal to 0%, and the upper bound is less than or equal to 100%. It also provides confidence intervals for facilities in which the survey estimates are zero (but other similarly conducted surveys could yield non-zero estimates).

Exposure period

To calculate comparative rates of sexual victimization, the facility provided the most recent admission date to the current facility for each youth. If the admission date was at least 12 months prior to the date of the survey, youth were asked questions related to their experiences during the last 12 months. If the admission date was less than 12 months prior to the interview, youth were asked about their experiences since they arrived at the facility. The average exposure period for sexual victimization among sampled youth was 6.2 months.

Measuring sexual victimization

The NSYC-2 relied on the reporting of direct experience of each youth, rather than youth reporting on the experience of other youth. The strategy was to first ask if the youth had engaged in any type of sexual activity at the facility within the last 12 months or since they entered the facility, if they had been in the facility for less than 12 months. These questions were not specific to the perpetrator or whether the sexual activity was coerced.

The initial series of questions differed by the age of the youth. Youth age 15 or older were administered questions related to the touching of body parts in a sexual way, involving oral, anal, or vaginal sex. Youth age 14 or younger were asked less detailed questions about sexual activity. Rather than referring to explicit body parts and acts, the items had less explicit language (i.e., "private parts"). This was done to avoid exposing younger respondents to explicit sexual references. (For specific survey questions, see appendix 1.)

Youth who reported sexual activity were then asked if the activities occurred with other youth or with staff. They were then asked questions about the presence and nature of coercion (including use of physical force or threat of physical force, use of other type of force or pressure, or return for money, favors, protection, or other special treatment) associated with the youth-on-youth sexual activity. A separate but identical set of questions was asked about coercion associated with staff-on-youth sexual activity. (See appendix 2.)

If the respondent did not report any sexual contact in the initial screening items, the ACASI survey administered a series of questions that asked if the youth had been coerced to engage in sexual activity. If a youth answered affirmatively, he or she was asked if the event occurred with another youth or with a staff member. Follow-up questions, comparable to the initial screener questions, were asked of those who reported victimization.

The ACASI survey presented additional questions related to both youth-on-youth and staff-on-youth sexual victimization. These questions collected further information on the characteristics of the victimization, such as time and location, number, race or Hispanic origin, and sex of perpetrators; injuries sustained and medical care received by the youth as a result of the assault; characteristics of the relationship between youth and staff perpetrators; and reporting of the assault to authorities and action taken by leadership after the victimization.

Measuring youth opinions about the facility staff and fairness of facility policies

The NSYC-1 and NSYC-2 included eight yes or no items that measured youth opinions about facility staff:

B1a. Are the facility staff good role models?

B1b. Are the facility staff friendly?

B1c. Do the staff seem to genuinely care about you?

B1d. Are the staff helpful?

B1e. Are the staff disrespectful?

B1f. Are the staff hard to get along with?

B1g. Are the staff mean?

B1h. Are the staff fun to be with?

"Yes" responses to items B1a, B1b, B1c, B1d, and B1h and "no" responses to items B1e, B1f, and B1g were coded 1. All other responses were coded 0. The response codes were then summed to provide a count of the number of positive opinions about the facility staff.

The number of positive opinions about the facility and fairness of facility policies was based on seven true or false items and one agree or disagree item:

B2a. Youth here are punished even when they don't do anything wrong.

B2b. Facility staff use force when they don't really need to.

B2c. Problems between facility staff and youth here can be worked out.

B2d. Something bad might happen to me if I file a complaint against a staff member.

B2e. I usually deserve any punishment that I receive.

B2f. Punishments given are fair.

B2g. The staff treat the youth fairly.

B2i. There are enough staff to monitor what is going on in this facility (strongly agree, somewhat agree, somewhat disagree, strongly disagree).

"False" responses to items B2a, B2b, and B2d and "true" responses to items B2c, B2e, B2f, and B2g were coded 1. "Strongly agree" and "somewhat agree" responses to item B2i were coded 1. All other responses were coded 0. The response codes were then summed to provide a count of the number of positive opinions about the facility and fairness of facility policies.

The entire ACASI questionnaire (listed as the National Survey of Youth in Custody-2) is available on the BJS website at www.bjs.gov.

The 13 facilities classified as high-rate were examined using additional exclusion criteria for extreme or inconsistent responses

The impact of the choice of exclusion criteria on the classification of high-rate facilities was examined (table 17). The data suggest that 10 of the 13 facilities would have remained in the high-rate group had additional (more restrictive) exclusion criteria been introduced.

One facility, John G. Richards (South Carolina), would have dropped out of the high-rate category if the calculations had excluded interviews in which youth reported a sexual victimization incident but failed to respond when asked how many times it had occurred or answered zero times. While the facility rate would have remained high (15.8%), the lower bound of the 95%-confidence interval (10 2%) would have been less than 135% of the national mean (less than 9.0% times 1.35, or 12.2%).

The John G. Richards facility also would have dropped out of the high-rate group if calculations had excluded interviews with two or more inconsistencies (with a mean of 15.8% and a lower bound of 10.2%) or if calculations had excluded interviews based on one or more inconsistencies (a mean of 8.6% and a lower bound of 4.4%).

Of the remaining 12 facilities, 2 facilities (Paulding Regional Youth Detention Center, Georgia, and Birchwood, South Carolina) would have dropped out only if interviews with any inconsistent response had been excluded. The rate of sexual victimization in the Paulding Regional Youth Detention Center would have dropped from 32.1% to 5.0%, and the rate at Birchwood from 29.2% to 4.6%. These two facilities had the smallest

Continued on next page

TABLE 17
Estimated rates of sexual victimization and lower bounds of the 95%-confidence intervals among high-rate facilities, by exclusion criteria, National Survey of Youth in Custody, 2012

Facility name	NSYC-2 final estimates — Extreme responses or 3 or more outliers[a] Percent	Lower bound	Number of times was zero or missing[b] Percent	Lower bound	Reported other sexual contacts only[c] Percent	Lower bound	2 or more outliers[d] Percent	Lower bound	1 or more outlier[e] Percent	Lower bound
All facilities - U.S. total	9.5%	8.7%	9.0%	8.3%	8.5%	7.8%	7.9%	7.2%	5.0%	4.5%
Paulding Reg. Yth. Det. Ctr. (GA)	32.1	21.7	29.6	19.2	29.6	19.2	24.0	14.1	5.0	1.2*
Circleville Juv. Corr. Fac. (OH)	30.3	24.4	29.2	23.4	29.2	23.4	27.0	21.1	19.2	13.0
Birchwood (SC)	29.2	20.6	29.2	21.0	26.1	17.8	22.7	14.5	10.5	4.6*
Eastman Yth. Dev. Campus (GA)	24.4	20.7	22.4	18.6	23.1	19.3	19.4	15.7	12.6	9.0
Scioto Juv. Corr. Fac. (OH)	23.2	18.1	22.1	16.6	20.9	15.5	20.9	15.5	16.4	11.1
Arkansas Juv. Assess. & Trtmt. Ctr. (AR)[f]	23.2	17.7	22.0	16.8	19.8	14.8	22.0	16.8	17.5	12.5
Corsicana Res. Trtmt. Ctr. (TX)[f]	22.4	17.1	22.4	17.2	20.3	15.3	19.2	14.2	15.9	10.7
Eldora State Training School for Boys (IA)	21.7	17.1	21.7	17.0	19.4	14.7	20.6	15.9	15.6	11.1
Illinois Yth. Ctr. Joliet (IL)	21.1	16.6	21.1	16.7	20.4	16.0	18.2	14.0	13.0	9.1
Augusta Yth. Dev. Campus (GA)	20.9	15.8	19.4	14.3	19.4	14.3	19.4	14.3	16.8	11.5
Sumter Yth. Dev. Campus (GA)	20.8	15.7	20.8	15.8	18.9	14.1	18.9	14.1	14.9	10.5
John G. Richards (SC)	20.0	14.1	15.8	10.2*	20.0	14.1	15.8	10.2*	8.6	4.4*
Cuyahoga Hills Juv. Corr. Fac. (OH)	19.8	14.6	19.0	13.8	19.0	13.8	19.0	13.8	13.1	8.3

Note: Additional exclusion criteria were designed to test if each facility remained in the high-rate category under various outlier scenarios related to data quality. (See *Methodology* for discussion of checks for extreme and inconsistent responses.) For a facility to be classified as high rate, the lower bound of the facility's 95%-confidence interval must exceed 1.35 times the national average. With the introduction of additional exclusion criteria, the threshold of 12.8% for the lower bound dropped to 12.2% (for zero or missing times), 11.5% (for exclusion of other sexual contacts only), 10.7% (for 2 or more outliers), and 6.8% (for 1 or more outlier).

*Facility would fall out of the high-rate group, based on the lower bound of its 95%-confidence interval.

[a]Final estimates based on the exclusion of 138 interviews with at least 1 extreme response or 3 or more inconsistent responses.

[b]Exclusion based on 1 or more extreme responses, 3 or more outliers, and youth who reported sexual victimization but failed to respond when asked "how many times" or responded with zero.

[c]Exclusion based on 1 or more extreme responses, 3 or more outliers, and youth who reported other sexual contacts only (e.g., kissing on the lips or other part of the body, looking at private body parts, showing something sexual, such as pictures or a movie, and engaging in some other sexual contact that did not involve touching).

[d]Exclusion based on 1 or more extreme responses and 2 or more outliers.

[e]Exclusion based on 1 or more extreme responses and 1 or more outliers.

[f]Facility housed both males and females. Both were sampled at this facility.

Source: Bureau of Justice Statistics, National Survey of Youth in Custody, 2012.

Continued from previous page

number of respondents (fewer than 30) among the 13 high-rate facilities, and consequently were the most sensitive to deleting interviews.

Consideration of other exclusion criteria did not change the classification of the remaining 10 facilities (not shown in table). These 10 remaining facilities would have been classified as high-rate even if interviews were dropped based on reports of an incident rate of more than one per week since the admission date or based on a case-by-case review of all items for internal consistency.

Overall, the data suggest that classifying the 13 facilities as high-rate is robust. In choosing to exclude interviews based on one or more extreme responses or three or more inconsistent responses, some youth may still report inconsistent information but their entire interview should not be invalidated.

Appendix 1. Survey items measuring sexual activity within the facility during the past 12 months or since entering the facility, if less than 12 months

Males, age 15 or older

C11. During the past 12 months, have you rubbed another person's penis with your hand or has someone rubbed your penis with their hand?

C12. During the past 12 months, have you rubbed another person's vagina with your hand?

C13. During the past 12 months, have you put your mouth on another person's penis or has someone put their mouth on your penis?

C14. During the past 12 months, have you put your mouth on someone's vagina?

C15. During the past 12 months, have you put your penis, finger, or something else inside someone else's rear end or has someone put their penis, finger, or something else inside your rear end?

C16. During the past 12 months, have you put your penis, finger, or something else inside someone's vagina?

C17. During the past 12 months, have you had any other kind of sexual contact with someone at this facility?

C17a. What kind of sexual contact was that?

CHECK ALL THAT APPLY.

Kissing on the lips 1

Kissing other parts of the body. . . 2

Looking at private parts. 3

Showing something sexual, such as pictures or a movie. 4

Something else that did not involve touching. 5

Something else that did involve touching. 6

Females, age 15 or older

C18. During the past 12 months, have you rubbed another person's penis with your hand?

C19. During the past 12 months, have you rubbed someone else's vagina with your hand or has someone else rubbed your vagina with their hand?

C20. During the past 12 months, have you put your mouth on another person's penis?

C21. During the past 12 months, have you put your mouth on someone else's vagina, or has someone put their mouth on your vagina?

C22. During the past 12 months, have you put your finger or something else inside someone else's rear end or has someone put their penis, finger, or something else inside your rear end?

C23. During the past 12 months, have you put your finger or something else inside someone else's vagina or has someone put their penis, finger, or something else inside your vagina?

C24. During the past 12 months, have you had any other kind of sexual contact with someone at this facility?

C24a. What kind of sexual contact was that?

CHECK ALL THAT APPLY.

Kissing on the lips 1

Kissing other parts of the body. . . 2

Looking at private parts. 3

Showing something sexual, such as pictures or a movie. 4

Something else that did not involve touching 5

Something else that did involve touching. 6

All youth age 14 or younger

C1. The next questions are about sexual contacts that happen in this facility.

Sexual contacts are when someone touches your private parts or you touch someone else's private parts in a sexual way.

By private parts, we mean any part of the body that would be covered by a bathing suit.

C11. During the past 12 months, have you rubbed anyone's private parts with your hand or has anyone rubbed your private parts with their hand?

C12. During the past 12 months, have you put your mouth on anyone's private parts or has anyone put their mouth on your private parts?

C13. During the past 12 months, have you put any part of your body inside anyone else's private parts?

C13a. During the past 12 months, has anyone put part of their body inside your private parts?

C14. During the past 12 months, have you had any other kind of sexual contact with someone at this facility?

C14a. What kind of sexual contact was that?

CHECK ALL THAT APPLY.

Kissing on the lips 1

Kissing other parts of the body. . . 2

Looking at private parts. 3

Showing something sexual, such as pictures or a movie. 4

Something else that did not involve touching 5

Something else that did involve touching. 6

Survey items measuring with whom the sexual activity occurred

C25. You've said that since you have been at this facility, you [list of specific activities]

Did (this/any of these) happen with a youth at this facility?

C27. During the past 12 months, which ones happened with a youth at this facility? [list of specific activities]

C28. You've said that since you have been at this facility, you [list of specific activities]

Did (this/any of these) happen with a member of the facility staff?

C30. During the past 12 months, which ones happened with a youth at this facility? [list of specific activities]

For incidents with youth

C31. During the past 12 months, did (this/any of these) ever happen because a youth at this facility used physical force or threat of physical force?

C34. During the past 12 months, did (this/any of these) ever happen because a youth at this facility forced or pressured you in some other way to do it?

C34a. How were you forced or pressured in some other way?

CHECK ALL THAT APPLY.

Another youth threatened you with harm 1

Another youth threatened to get you in trouble with other youth . 2

Another youth threatened to get you in trouble with the staff 3

Another youth kept asking you to do it. 4

Another youth forced or pressured you in some other way. 5

C36. During the past 12 months, did (this/any of these) ever happen with a youth at this facility in return for money, favors, protection, or other special treatment?

For incidents with staff

C45. During the past 12 months, did (this/any of these) ever happen because a staff member used physical force or threat of physical force?

C48. During the past 12 months, did (this/any of these) ever happen because a staff member forced or pressured you in some other way to do it?

C48a. How were you forced or pressured in some other way?

CHECK ALL THAT APPLY.

A staff member threatened you with harm 1

A staff member threatened to get you in trouble with other youth . . 2

A staff member threatened to get you in trouble with the staff 3

A staff member kept asking you to do it 4

A staff member forced or pressured you in some other way 5

C50. During the past 12 months, did (this/any of these) ever happen with a staff member in return for money, favors, protection, or other special treatment?

Items unrelated to reports of sexual victimization

1. Reported one of the following:

- being admitted to the facility before turning age 8

- being admitted to the facility in the future

- being 8 feet tall or taller

- weighing 500 pounds or more

- having a Body Mass Index of either less than 15 or 50 or greater.

2. Youth "strongly agreed" with the statement "that some of the questions about sexual activity were hard to understand."

3. Youth reported being sexually assaulted prior to admission to the facility, but when asked "how many times," reported "0."

4./5. Youth reported being physically assaulted by staff/youth more than 3 times per day.

6./7. Youth reported being physically assaulted by staff/youth, but when asked "how many times," responded with "0."

8./9. Youth reported being injured by staff/youth, but when asked "how many times," responded with "0."

Items related to reports of sexual victimization

10. Youth reported sexual contact with a staff member, but the type of activity was not consistent with the sex of the perpetrator reported during the interview.

11. Youth reported sexual assault by another youth, but the type of activity was not consistent with the sex of the perpetrator reported during the interview.

12./13. Reports of injury resulting from sexual assault by staff/youth were not consistently reported in different sections of the questionnaire.

14./15. Responses about reporting a sexual assault by staff/youth to the facility administrators were not consistent across different questions of the questionnaire.

16./17. Youth reported forced sexual contact by staff/youth in one section, but did not report specific types of coercion in another section of the questionnaire.

18./19. Youth reported having sexual contact with staff or forced sexual contact with youth, but did not provide the specific type of activity that occurred.[1]

---

[1]Response choices added in the NSYC-2 questionnaire provided youth with the option of selecting "pressured or hurt in some other way."

20./21. Youth did not provide details about a report of injury resulting from forced sexual contact with staff/youth.

22./23. Youth reported sexual penetration by staff/youth in one section of the questionnaire but not in another section.

24./25. Youth reported having sexual contact with staff/youth, but when asked "how many times," responded with "0."

26./27. Youth reported sexual contact with staff/youth in return for money, favors, protection, or special treatment at the time of sexual contact in one section, but did not report these in another section of the questionnaire.

28. Youth reported being told of staff's personal life or receiving special treatment by staff in one section, but reported the opposite in another section of the questionnaire.

29. Youth reported not being told of staff's personal life or not receiving special treatment by staff in one section, but reported the opposite in another section of the questionnaire.

30. Youth reported an extreme number of sexual assaults (e.g., 999, 9999) or a number with non-quantitative significance (e.g., 69, 666).

Characteristics of juvenile facilities participating in the National Survey of Youth in Custody, 2012

Facility name	Number of sampled youth	Number of ineligible youth[b]	Number of respondents[a]		Response rate[c]
			All completed NSYC-2 interviews	Sexual victimization survey	
All facilities - U.S. total	16,500	6,444	9,703	8,707	58.9%
Alabama					
Mt. Meigs Campus	148	15	98	88	66.2%
Troy University Group Home[e]	2	3	2	2	100
Vacca Campus	56	14	48	44	86.3
Alaska					
Fairbanks Yth. Fac.[f]	17	5	14	13	86.7%
Johnson Yth. Ctr.[f]	15	4	15	13	100
McLaughlin Yth. Ctr. Det. & Training[f]	91	14	83	75	91.5
Arizona					
Adobe Mountain School[d]	160	184	110	100	69.4%
Black Canyon School[f]	62	55	55	49	87.5
Arkansas					
Arkansas Juv. Assess. & Trtmt. Ctr.[f,g]	92	24	78	70	84.3%
Colt Juv. Trtmt. Ctr.	27	3	24	21	87.5
Dermott Juv. Corr. Fac.	43	2	36	33	84.6
Garland Co. Juv. Det. Ctr.[f,g]	7	21	7	7	100
Harrisburg Juv. Trtmt. Ctr.	33	9	29	26	89.7
Jefferson Co. Juv. Det. Ctr.[f,g]	21	57	10	10	52.6
Lewisville Juv. Trtmt. Ctr.[g]	29	6	24	22	81.5
Mansfield Juv. Trtmt. Ctr.	23	9	22	19	95.0
Mansfield Juv. Trtmt. Ctr. for Girls[e]	15	3	14	12	92.3
Yell Co. Juv. Det. Ctr.[f]	11	45	11	10	100
California					
N.A. Chaderjian Yth. Corr. Fac.	281	70	60	51	20.2%
O.H. Close Yth. Corr. Fac.	219	23	60	53	26.9
Pine Grove Yth. Conservation Camp	62	16	15	14	25.0
Ventura Yth. Corr. Fac.[d,f]	230	118	55	49	23.7
Colorado					
Betty Marler Yth. Srvcs. Ctr.[e,g]	36	1	33	29	90.6%
Grand Mesa Yth. Srvcs. Ctr.[f]	39	12	37	33	94.3
Lookout Mtn. Yth. Srvcs. Ctr.	147	9	129	115	87.1
Mt. View Yth. Srvcs. Ctr.[f]	63	22	47	42	75.0
Platte Valley Yth. Srvcs. Ctr.[f]	59	9	51	46	86.8
Ridge View Acad.[d,g]	158	86	123	110	77.5
Spring Creek Yth. Srvcs. Ctr.[f]	27	12	25	23	92.0
Synergy Adolescent Trtmt. Prog.	13	6	7	6	50.0
Zebulon Pike Yth. Srvcs. Ctr.	33	4	28	26	86.7
Connecticut					
Connecticut Juv. Training School	105	20	16	15	16.0%
Delaware					
Ferris School	39	3	24	21	60.0%
Snowden Cottage	11	3	9	8	80.0
District of Columbia					
New Beginnings Yth. Dev. Ctr.	46	15	27	24	57.1%
Florida					
Big Cypress Wilderness Inst.[f,g]	28	1	6	6	24.0%
Brevard Group Trtmt. Home[g]	22	9	5	4	20.0
Bristol Yth. Acad.	51	19	24	21	46.7
Britt Halfway House	27	4	8	7	29.2
Camp E-Nini-Hassee[e,g]	16	6	7	6	42.9
Challenge Juv. Res. Fac.[g]	56	10	16	14	28.0
Columbus Juv. Res. Fac.[g]	48	4	7	6	14.0
Cypress Creek Juv. Offender Corr. Ctr.	93	14	55	48	57.1
Dade Juv. Res. Fac.[g]	55	8	23	20	40.8

Characteristics of juvenile facilities participating in the National Survey of Youth in Custody, 2012

Facility name	Number of sampled youth	Number of ineligible youth[b]	Number of respondents[a]		Response rate[c]
			All completed NSYC-2 interviews	Sexual victimization survey	
Daytona Juv. Res. Fac.	22	8	7	6	30.0%
Duval Halfway House	21	12	9	8	42.1
Falkenburg Juv. Corr. Fac. - Mental Health	59	7	32	29	54.7
Florida Environmental Inst.[g]	14	2	8	7	58.3
Ft. Walton Adolescent Substance Abuse Prog.[g]	43	4	9	8	21.1
Gulf & Lake Acad.[f,g]	66	17	15	14	23.3
Hastings Comprehensive Mental Health Trtmt. Prog.[g]	88	13	43	38	47.5
JoAnn Bridges Acad.[e]	20	4	12	11	61.1
Kissimmee Juv. Corr. Fac.	31	3	9	8	28.6
Les Peters Halfway House	18	12	9	9	56.3
Marion Juv. Corr. Fac.	37	8	14	13	38.2
Milton Girls Juv. Res. Fac.[e]	56	8	18	16	32.0
Okaloosa Yth. Acad.	72	13	13	12	18.5
Okeechobee Intensive Halfway House[g]	27	6	8	8	32.0
Okeechobee Juv. Offender Corr. Ctr.	83	9	55	50	66.7
Okeechobee Yth. Dev. Ctr.[g]	116	27	48	43	41.0
Orange Yth. Acad.[g]	43	10	16	16	41.0
Palm Beach Juv. Corr. Fac.	111	5	46	41	41.0
Palmetto Yth. Acad.	47	6	28	25	58.1
Pensacola Boys Base	20	2	12	11	61.1
Polk Halfway House[g]	22	3	7	6	31.6
Thompson Acad.	131	39	24	21	17.8
Tiger Success Ctr.	22	4	8	7	35.0
Union Juv. Res. Fac.	18	1	7	6	37.5
Volusia Halfway House	18	7	7	7	41.2
WINGS for Life[e]	10	3	5	5	55.6
Yth. Environmental Srvcs.[g]	33	4	16	16	53.3
Georgia					
Aaron Cohn Reg. Yth. Det. Ctr.[f]	28	104	13	12	48.0%
Albany Reg. Yth. Det. Ctr.[f]	3	46	3	3	100
Augusta Reg. Yth. Det. Ctr.	36	46	22	20	60.6
Augusta Yth. Dev. Campus	69	13	57	51	82.3
Bob Richards Reg. Yth. Det. Ctr.[f]	35	72	12	11	34.4
Crisp Yth. Det. Ctr.	27	95	18	16	64.0
Eastman Reg. Yth. Det. Ctr.	14	58	10	9	75.0
Eastman Yth. Dev. Campus	156	38	128	116	82.9
Gainesville Reg. Yth. Det. Ctr.[f]	25	109	18	16	72.7
Gwinnett Reg. Yth. Det. Ctr.[f]	24	61	14	12	57.1
Macon Reg. Yth. Det. Ctr.	18	113	14	12	75.0
Macon Yth. Dev. Campus[e]	58	65	39	37	69.8
Muscogee Yth. Dev. Ctr.	59	11	49	44	83.0
Paulding Reg. Yth. Det. Ctr.	57	117	33	29	56.9
Savannah Reg. Yth. Det. Ctr.[f]	46	150	19	17	41.5
Sumter Yth. Dev. Campus	144	15	97	87	67.4
Waycross Reg. Yth. Det. Ctr.[f]	7	76	6	5	83.3
Hawaii					
Hawaii Yth. Corr. Fac.[f]	53	7	42	37	78.7%
Idaho					
Juv. Corr. Ctr. - Lewiston	32	4	30	27	93.1%
Juv. Corr. Ctr. - Nampa[f]	69	21	60	53	85.5
Juv. Corr. Ctr. - St. Anthony[f]	122	13	116	104	94.5
Three Springs of Mountain Home[g,h]	0	37	0	0	0.0

Characteristics of juvenile facilities participating in the National Survey of Youth in Custody, 2012

| Facility name | Number of sampled youth | Number of ineligible youth[b] | Number of respondents[a] | | Response rate[c] |
			All completed NSYC-2 interviews	Sexual victimization survey	
Illinois					
Illinois Yth. Ctr. - Chicago	58	47	41	37	71.2%
Illinois Yth. Ctr. - Harrisburg[d]	164	188	117	102	68.9
Illinois Yth. Ctr. - Joliet[d]	168	107	129	115	75.7
Illinois Yth. Ctr. - Kewanee[d]	161	82	127	115	79.3
Illinois Yth. Ctr. - St. Charles	87	57	65	59	75.6
Illinois Yth. Ctr. - Warrenville[e]	41	20	26	23	62.2
Illinois Yth. Ctr. - Pere Marquette	14	26	11	10	76.9
Indiana					
Camp Summit Boot Camp	86	2	79	70	90.9%
Logansport Juv. Corr. Fac./Trtmt. Unit	102	16	95	85	92.4
Madison Juv. Corr. Fac.[e]	44	27	40	36	90.0
Pendleton Juv. Corr. Fac.[d]	160	56	126	113	78.5
South Bend Juv. Corr. Fac.	82	17	74	66	89.2
Iowa					
Eldora State Training School for Boys	96	7	76	69	80.2%
Girls State Training School[f]	12	1	10	9	81.8
Woodlands Trtmt. Ctr.[f,g]	16	0	16	14	100
Woodward Acad.[d,g]	160	74	137	122	84.7
Kansas					
Judge Riddel Boys Ranch[g]	37	9	35	31	93.9%
Juv. Det. Ctr.[f,g]	19	15	16	14	82.4
Kansas Juv. Corr. Complex[d,f]	158	117	136	122	85.9
Larned Juv. Corr. Fac.	100	23	93	83	92.2
Shawnee Co. Juv. Det. Ctr.[f,g]	22	24	18	16	80.0
Kentucky					
Adair Yth. Dev. Ctr.[f]	23	7	18	16	76.2%
Audubon Yth. Dev. Ctr.	30	9	22	19	70.4
Cadet Leadership & Education Program	20	0	20	18	100
Green River Yth. Dev. Ctr.	20	11	20	18	100
Lake Cumberland Yth. Dev. Ctr.	27	8	23	21	87.5
Lincoln Village Yth. Dev. Ctr. & Reg. Juv. Det.[f]	26	0	19	18	78.3
London Group Home	7	1	7	6	100
Mayfield Yth. Dev. Ctr.	30	2	24	22	81.5
McCracken Reg. Juv. Det. Ctr.[f]	6	10	6	5	100
Morehead Yth. Dev. Ctr.[f]	29	5	27	24	92.3
Northern Kentucky Yth. Dev. Ctr.	34	3	31	28	90.3
Owensboro Trtmt. Ctr.	24	1	24	22	100
Warren Reg. Juv. Det.[f]	5	19	5	5	100
Louisiana					
A. B. Horn Group Home, Harmony Ctr. Inc.[g]	4	4	4	4	100%
Boys & Girls Villages[f,g]	22	3	7	7	35.0
Bridge City Ctr. for Yth.	129	12	77	69	59.5
Christian Acres[f,g]	53	11	26	24	50.0
Jetson Corr. Ctr. for Yth.	85	4	32	30	39.5
Johnny Robinson Boys Home[g]	20	6	4	4	22.2
Louisiana Methodist Children's Home[f,g]	17	4	6	6	37.5
Rutherford House[g]	36	17	19	16	50.0
Swanson Ctr. for Yth.	124	48	43	38	34.2
Ware Yth. Ctr.[f,g]	97	36	32	28	32.2
Maine					
Long Creek Yth. Dev. Ctr.[f]	69	4	57	52	83.9%
Mtn. View Yth. Dev. Ctr.	57	13	44	38	74.5

Characteristics of juvenile facilities participating in the National Survey of Youth in Custody, 2012

Facility name	Number of sampled youth	Number of ineligible youth[b]	Number of respondents[a]		
			All completed NSYC-2 interviews	Sexual victimization survey	Response rate[c]
Maryland					
Backbone Mountain Yth. Ctr.	44	21	10	9	23.1%
Baltimore City Juv. Justice Ctr.	40	25	4	3	8.3
Charles H. Hickey, Jr. School	13	29	1	1	8.3
Cheltenham Yth. Fac.	39	59	1	1	2.8
Green Ridge Yth. Ctr.	40	9	10	9	25.0
Meadow Mountain Yth. Ctr.	36	17	13	12	37.5
Savage Mountain Yth. Ctr.	32	15	5	4	13.8
Victor Cullen Ctr.	47	10	14	12	28.6
Massachusetts					
Alliance House[g]	6	2	4	4	80.0%
Bishop Ruocco House Trtmt. Ctr.[e,g]	5	6	2	2	50.0
Brewster Trtmt.	5	9	3	3	75.0
Ctr. for Human Dev. Adolescent Trtmt. Program[g]	12	4	6	6	54.5
Fay A. Rotenberg School [e,g]	7	4	6	5	83.3
Gandara Hispanic Group Home, Gandara Mental Health Ctr. [g]	8	3	7	6	85.7
Goss Secure Trtmt. #1	16	4	9	8	53.3
Goss Secure Trtmt. #2, Taunton Hospital	15	6	5	5	35.7
Judge Connelly Yth. Ctr.	11	1	4	3	33.3
Kennedy School, RFK Children's Action Corps.	9	3	6	5	62.5
Phaneuf Ctr.[g]	14	2	13	12	92.3
Spectrum R.E.A.C.H. Program[d]	11	6	7	7	70.0
Springfield Secure Res. Trtmt. Prog.[g]	15	0	6	6	42.9
Westboro Reception	6	15	2	2	40.0
Westboro Secure Trtmt.	11	1	9	8	80.0
Worcester Secure Trtmt. Ctr.	9	4	6	5	62.5
Michigan					
Bay Pines Ctr.[f]	33	4	22	20	66.7%
Clinton Campus[g]	62	16	12	10	18.2
W.J. Maxey Boys Training School	32	12	23	21	75.0
Shawono Ctr.	25	2	9	9	40.9
Minnesota					
Minnesota Corr. Fac. - Red Wing[d]	106	21	56	52	54.7%
Minnesota Corr. Fac. - Togo[f]	21	11	5	5	26.3
Southwestern Yth. Srvcs.[g]	16	10	5	4	28.6
Mississippi					
Oakley Yth. Dev. Ctr.[f]	54	0	47	42	87.5%
Missouri					
Babler Lodge	7	8	6	6	100%
Bissell Hall	13	6	9	8	66.7
Camp Avery	26	3	26	24	100
Datema House	6	8	6	6	100
Delmina Woods Yth. Fac.[e]	23	0	20	17	85.0
Discovery Hall[e]	12	0	10	9	81.8
Ft. Bellefontaine Campus	25	1	25	23	100
Fulton Trtmt. Ctr.	27	3	23	20	83.3
Gentry Res. Trtmt. Ctr.	20	3	18	16	88.9
Girardot Ctr. for Yth. & Family	19	1	18	16	94.1
Green Gables Lodge	8	1	8	7	100
Hillsboro Trtmt. Ctr.	27	1	22	19	79.2
Hogan Street Reg. Yth. Ctr.	30	4	26	23	85.2
Montgomery City Yth. Ctr.	37	1	36	32	97.0
Mount Vernon Trtmt. Ctr.	30	5	29	26	96.3
Northwest Reg. Yth. Ctr.	25	0	20	18	78.3
New Madrid Bend Yth. Ctr.	17	5	15	14	93.3

Characteristics of juvenile facilities participating in the National Survey of Youth in Custody, 2012

Facility name	Number of sampled youth	Number of ineligible youth[b]	Number of respondents[a]		Response rate[c]
			All completed NSYC-2 interviews	Sexual victimization survey	
Northeast Community Trtmt. Ctr.	12	0	11	9	90.0%
Rich Hill Yth. Dev. Ctr.	19	3	19	17	100
Riverbend Trtmt. Ctr.	26	2	23	22	95.7
Rosa Parks Ctr.[e]	8	2	8	7	100
Sierra-Osage Trtmt. Ctr.[f]	21	0	19	17	89.5
Spanish Lake Campus	25	1	20	19	86.4
Twin Rivers Campus[e]	17	3	14	13	81.3
W.E. Sears Yth. Ctr.	51	6	47	42	91.3
Watkins Mill Park Camp[f]	56	8	51	45	90.0
Waverly Reg. Yth. Ctr.	41	1	38	34	91.9
Wilson Creek	9	7	9	8	100
Montana					
Pine Hills Yth. Corr. Fac.	64	13	25	23	39.7%
Yth. Transition Ctr.[f]	7	4	2	2	28.6
Nebraska					
Yth. Rehab. & Trtmt. Ctr. - Geneva[e]	78	23	27	24	34.3%
Yth. Rehab. & Trtmt. Ctr. - Kearney	142	62	30	29	22.7
Nevada					
Caliente Yth. Ctr.[f]	116	28	47	42	40.4%
Nevada Yth. Training Ctr.	79	9	37	33	46.5
New Hampshire					
John H. Sununu Yth. Srvcs. Ctr.[f]	57	15	6	6	11.5%
Orion House[g]	6	6	1	1	16.7
New Jersey					
Albert Elias Res. Community Home	8	6	7	6	85.7%
D.O.V.E.S. Res. Community Home[e]	5	1	5	5	100
Essex Res. Community Home	11	14	7	6	60.0
Fresh Start	13	8	8	7	58.3
Juv. Female Secure Care & Intake Fac.[e]	16	6	7	6	40.0
Juv. Medium Security Fac.	66	50	21	19	32.2
New Jersey Training School & Intake Fac.	194	109	80	72	41.4
Ocean Res. Community Home	23	12	14	12	60.0
Southern Res. Community Home	18	12	7	6	37.5
Vineland Prep Acad.	28	43	17	15	60.0
Voorhees Res. Community Home	14	2	6	6	50.0
Warren Res. Community Home	20	1	16	14	77.8
New Mexico					
Albuquerque Boys' Ctr.	10	0	7	7	77.8%
Camino Nuevo Yth. Ctr.[f]	70	34	49	44	69.8
J. Paul Taylor Ctr.	48	4	23	21	48.8
Yth. Diagnostic & Dev. Ctr. (Males)	84	5	31	30	39.0
New York					
Brentwood Res. Ctr.[e]	16	2	0	0	0.0%
Bronx Res. Ctr.[f]	20	5	0	0	0.0
Brookwood Secure Ctr.	123	14	27	22	20.0
Finger Lakes Res. Ctr.	64	22	2	2	3.4
Goshen Secure Ctr.[f]	62	6	12	12	21.4
Highland Res. Ctr.	76	27	9	8	11.6
Industry Res. Ctr.	40	26	1	1	2.8
Lansing Res. Ctr.	16	10	0	0	0.0
MacCormick Secure Ctr.	24	3	1	1	4.5
Middletown Res. Ctr.	29	3	2	2	7.7
Red Hook Res. Ctr.	16	6	1	1	6.7
Sgt. Henry Johnson Yth. Leadership Acad.	26	5	2	2	8.7
Staten Island Res. Ctr.	14	11	0	0	0.0

Characteristics of juvenile facilities participating in the National Survey of Youth in Custody, 2012

Facility name	Number of sampled youth	Number of ineligible youth[b]	Number of respondents[a]		
			All completed NSYC-2 interviews	Sexual victimization survey	Response rate[c]
North Carolina					
C.A. Dillon Yth. Dev. Ctr.	75	19	40	35	52.2%
Chatham Yth. Dev. Ctr.[f]	27	0	13	11	45.8
Dobbs Yth. Dev. Ctr.	25	4	9	8	34.8
Edgecombe Yth. Dev. Ctr.	25	6	6	6	26.1
Lenoir Yth. Dev. Ctr.	25	4	7	7	30.4
Stonewall Jackson Yth. Dev. Ctr.	91	22	42	38	46.3
North Dakota					
Dakota Boys & Girls Ranch (Minot)[f,g]	10	1	9	8	88.9
North Dakota Yth. Corr. Ctr.[f]	48	27	41	37	86.0%
Prairie Learning Ctr.[f,g]	13	7	10	9	90.0
Ohio					
Circleville Juv. Corr. Fac.	95	9	76	66	77.6%
Cuyahoga Hills Juv. Corr. Fac.[d]	144	54	102	89	68.5
Indian River Juv. Corr. Fac.	145	31	117	105	80.8
Scioto Juv. Corr. Fac.[f]	111	52	75	69	69.0
Oklahoma					
Cedar Canyon[g]	15	5	4	3	23.1%
Central Oklahoma Juv. Ctr.[f]	75	5	13	10	14.9
Foss Lake Adventure Program	13	12	7	6	50.0
Lawton Adventure Program	13	6	3	3	25.0
Southwest Oklahoma Juv. Ctr. (Manitou)	61	11	22	20	36.4
Tenkiller	11	6	4	4	40.0
Oregon					
Camp Florence Yth. Transition Fac.	23	2	21	19	90.5%
Camp Tillamook Yth. Transition Fac.	22	1	20	18	94.7
Eastern Oregon Yth. Corr. Fac.	52	5	51	45	97.8
Hillcrest Yth. Corr. Fac.	143	27	125	114	88.4
MacLaren Yth. Corr. Fac.	174	17	138	122	78.2
North Coast Yth. Corr. Fac.	48	4	43	38	88.4
Oak Creek Yth. Corr. Fac.[e]	50	4	44	39	86.7
RiverBend Yth. Transition Fac.	44	11	36	32	80.0
Rogue Valley Yth. Corr. Fac.	105	8	101	90	95.7
Tillamook Yth. Corr. Fac.	51	2	49	44	95.7
Pennsylvania					
Cresson Secure Trtmt. Unit[d]	25	8	9	9	40.9%
Loysville Yth. Dev. Ctr.	80	18	34	30	41.7
New Castle Yth. Dev. Ctr. Adolescent Sexual Offenders Program	19	3	11	10	55.6
New Castle Yth. Dev. Ctr. Secure Trtmt. Program	32	15	13	11	37.9
North Central Secure Trtmt.	55	9	27	23	46.9
North Central Secure Trtmt. Unit, Girls Program - Reed Building[e]	27	4	20	18	75.0
South Mountain Secure Trtmt. Unit	25	3	9	8	36.4
Yth. Forestry Camp #2	25	14	15	14	60.9
Yth. Forestry Camp #3	32	17	18	16	57.1
Rhode Island					
Thomas C. Slater Training School for Yth.[f]	74	39	43	39	59.1%
South Carolina					
AMIkids Beaufort[g]	19	3	17	15	88.2%
Birchwood	34	10	29	25	83.3
Camp Aspen	32	9	31	28	96.6
John G. Richards	57	8	45	40	76.9
Willow Lane[e]	9	3	8	7	87.5

Characteristics of juvenile facilities participating in the National Survey of Youth in Custody, 2012

Facility name	Number of sampled youth	Number of ineligible youth[b]	Number of respondents[a]		Response rate[c]
			All completed NSYC-2 interviews	Sexual victimization survey	
South Dakota					
Adolescent Sexual Adjustment Program[f,g]	24	2	16	14	63.6%
Chamberlain Acad.[f,g]	9	9	5	4	50.0
Excel Program[e]	13	8	4	3	25.0
Parkston Res. Trtmt. Program[f,g]	17	2	6	5	33.3
Patrick Henry Brady Acad.	38	22	11	9	26.5
Yth. Challenge Ctr.	37	11	11	10	30.3
Tennessee					
John S. Wilder Yth. Dev. Ctr.	103	29	39	35	37.6%
Mountain View Yth. Dev. Ctr.	95	27	38	33	38.8
New Visions[e]	17	7	6	6	37.5
Taft Yth. Dev. Ctr.	50	25	26	23	51.1
Woodland Hills Yth. Dev. Ctr.	114	26	49	43	42.2
Texas					
Ayres House	15	2	13	11	84.6%
Corsicana Res. Trtmt. Ctr.	119	0	85	76	71.0
Cottrell House	17	11	12	10	66.7
Evins Reg. Juv. Ctr.	138	2	79	70	56.0
Gainesville State School[d]	160	134	117	106	73.6
Giddings State School[d]	160	137	120	106	73.6
McFadden Ranch	41	9	32	29	78.4
McLennan Co. State Juv. Corr. Fac.[d]	160	168	116	106	73.6
Ron Jackson State Juv. Corr. Complex Unit I[e]	103	15	89	84	90.3
Schaeffer House	13	4	13	12	100
Turman House	17	6	11	11	68.8
Willoughby House[e]	14	3	14	12	100
Utah					
Co. Res. Group Home[g]	5	11	3	2	50.0%
Decker Lake Yth. Ctr.	29	6	20	18	69.2
Millcreek Yth. Ctr.[d,f]	58	23	38	33	63.5
Odyssey House Adolescent Fac.[f,g]	14	3	8	7	58.3
Slate Canyon Yth. Ctr.	17	7	10	9	60.0
Turning Point Family Care[g]	13	0	5	5	41.7
Wasatch Yth. Ctr.	32	11	15	13	46.4
Yth. Health Associates (West, East, North Group Homes)	43	4	14	13	33.3
Vermont					
Woodside Juv. Rehab. Ctr.[f]	17	5	16	15	93.8%
Virginia					
Beaumont Juv. Corr. Ctr.	209	43	76	68	36.2%
Bon Air Juv. Corr. Ctr.[f]	155	36	48	45	32.4
Culpeper Juv. Corr. Ctr.[f]	114	20	65	61	59.2
Hanover Juv. Corr. Ctr.	53	20	17	15	31.3
Newport News Juv. Det.[h]	0	38	0	0	0.0
Washington					
Canyon View Community Fac.	6	10	3	3	50.0%
Echo Glen Children's Ctr.[f]	153	23	41	37	26.8
Green Hill School[d]	179	67	79	69	43.1
Juv. Offender Basic Training Camp[f]	8	17	2	2	28.6
Naselle Yth. Camp	96	26	40	35	40.7
Oakridge State Community Fac.	14	3	10	9	75.0
Parke Creek Trtmt. Ctr.	8	12	3	3	42.9
Ridgeview Group Home	6	4	2	2	40.0

Characteristics of juvenile facilities participating in the National Survey of Youth in Custody, 2012

Facility name	Number of sampled youth	Number of ineligible youth[b]	Number of respondents[a]		
			All completed NSYC-2 interviews	Sexual victimization survey	Response rate[c]
West Virginia					
Davis Stuart Lewisburg Main Campus Res. Prog.[h]	0	27	0	0	0.0
Kenneth Honey Rubenstein Juv. Ctr.	41	2	40	36	97.3%
West Virginia Industrial Home for Yth.[f]	84	2	81	73	96.1
Wisconsin					
Copper Lake School[e]	22	4	19	17	85.0%
Lincoln Hills School[d]	165	145	123	110	73.8
Mendota Juv. Trtmt. Ctr.	29	5	23	21	80.8
Wyoming					
Wyoming Boys' School	70	20	41	37	58.7%
Wyoming Girls' School[e]	40	7	21	19	52.8

Note: A total of 9,073 youth participated in NSYC-2. Approximately 10% (996) were randomly assigned to the survey on alcohol and drug use and treatment. Facilities housed males only unless otherwise noted.

[a]Number of adjudicated youth who participated in the survey. Includes 40 youth who reported on some of the sexual victimization questions but not all of them.

[b]Youth were considered ineligible if they were mentally or physically incapacitated, admitted to the facility within 2 weeks prior to the data collection period, transferred or released after sample selection but before the data collection period, or excluded based on subsampling within the facility. (See *Methodology*.)

[c]Response rate accounts for different probabilities of selection among youth and the exclusion of interviews with extreme or inconsistent responses. (See *Methodology*.)

[d]Youth subsampled after initial sample was selected.

[e]Facility housed females only.

[f]Facility housed both males and females. Both were sampled at this facility.

[g]Facility held state-placed youth, but was not state-owned or -operated.

[h]Facility was sampled but not visited due to issues related to scheduling and burden.

Source: Bureau of Justice Statistics, National Survey of Youth in Custody, 2012.

APPENDIX TABLE 2
Percent of youth reporting sexual victimization, by facility, National Survey of Youth in Custody, 2012

Facility name	Percent of youth reporting any sexual victimization		
		95%-confidence interval	
	Weighted percent[a]	Lower bound	Upper bound
All facilities - U.S. total	9.5%	8.7%	10.3%
Alabama			
Mt. Meigs Campus	12.2%	8.5%	17.1%
Vacca Campus	15.9	11.3	21.9
Alaska			
McLaughlin Yth. Ctr. Det. & Training[c]	5.3%	3.5%	7.9%
Arizona			
Adobe Mountain School[e]	10.1%	6.4%	15.7%
Black Canyon School[c,e]	4.2	2.2	7.7
Arkansas			
Arkansas Juv. Assess. & Trtmt. Ctr.[c,d]	23.2%	17.7%	29.7%
Colt Juv. Trtmt. Ctr.	19.0	12.0	28.9
Dermott Juv. Corr. Fac.	12.1	7.5	18.9
Harrisburg Juv. Trtmt. Ctr.	7.7	4.0	14.2
Lewisville Juv. Trtmt. Ctr.[d]	9.1	4.4	17.9
Mansfield Juv. Trtmt. Ctr.	5.3	2.2	12.0
California[f]			
Colorado			
Betty Marler Yth. Srvcs. Ctr.[b,d]	17.2%	12.1%	23.9%
Grand Mesa Yth. Srvcs. Ctr.[c]	0.0	0.0	1.9
Lookout Mtn. Yth. Srvcs. Ctr.	7.8	5.7	10.7
Mt. View Yth. Srvcs. Ctr.[c]	0.0	0.0	3.1
Platte Valley Yth. Srvcs. Ctr.[c,e]	8.9	5.6	13.9
Ridge View Acad.[d]	9.6	6.3	14.3
Spring Creek Yth. Srvcs. Ctr.[c]	13.0	8.7	19.1
Zebulon Pike Yth. Srvcs. Ctr.	11.5	6.8	19.0
Connecticut[f]			
Delaware			
Ferris School	0.0%	0.0%	8.4%
District of Columbia			
New Beginnings Yth. Dev. Ctr.	0.0%	0.0%	8.5%
Florida			
Bristol Yth. Acad.	10.7%	3.2%	30.2%
Cypress Creek Juv. Offender Corr. Ctr.	4.7	1.7	12.4
Falkenburg Juv. Corr. Fac. - Mental Health	4.2	1.6	10.8
Hastings Comprehensive Mental Health Trtmt. Fac.[d]	6.0	2.1	15.9
Okeechobee Juv. Offender Corr. Ctr.	7.6	3.6	15.5
Okeechobee Yth. Dev. Ctr.[d]	2.6	0.9	7.6
Palm Beach Juv. Corr. Fac.	16.2	7.3	32.1
Palmetto Yth. Acad.	0.0	0.0	8.2
Georgia			
Augusta Reg. Yth. Det. Ctr.	5.0%	1.4%	16.8%
Augusta Yth. Dev. Campus	20.9	15.8	27.1
Crisp Yth. Det. Ctr.	12.5	5.1	27.5
Eastman Yth. Dev. Campus[e]	24.4	20.7	28.5
Gainesville Reg. Yth. Det. Ctr.[c]	12.5	5.4	26.5
Macon Yth. Dev. Campus[b]	5.1	2.2	11.4
Muscogee Yth. Dev. Ctr.	6.8	3.8	12.0
Paulding Reg. Yth. Det. Ctr.[e]	32.1	21.7	44.7
Sumter Yth. Dev. Campus[e]	20.8	15.7	27.0
Hawaii			
Hawaii Yth. Corr. Fac.[c]	10.8%	6.3%	17.9%
Idaho			
Juv. Corr. Ctr. - Lewiston	3.7%	1.7%	8.0%
Juv. Corr. Ctr. - Nampa[c]	3.8	1.9	7.2
Juv. Corr. Ctr. - St. Anthony[c]	3.8	2.7	5.5

Percent of youth reporting sexual victimization, by facility, National Survey of Youth in Custody, 2012

Facility name	Weighted percent[a]	Percent of youth reporting any sexual victimization	
		95%-confidence interval	
		Lower bound	Upper bound
Illinois			
Illinois Yth. Ctr. - Chicago	13.5%	8.1%	21.7%
Illinois Yth. Ctr. - Harrisburg	15.7	10.5	22.7
Illinois Yth. Ctr. - Joliet	21.1	16.6	26.3
Illinois Yth. Ctr. - Kewanee	14.8	11.0	19.8
Illinois Yth. Ctr. - St. Charles	5.1	2.7	9.5
Illinois Yth. Ctr. - Warrenville[b]	13.0	6.1	25.6
Indiana			
Camp Summit Boot Camp	2.9%	1.6%	5.2%
Logansport Juv. Corr. Fac./Trtmt. Unit	9.4	7.2	12.2
Madison Juv. Corr. Fac.[b]	8.3	5.2	13.2
Pendleton Juv. Corr. Fac.[e]	13.5	9.6	18.6
South Bend Juv. Corr. Fac.	13.6	10.1	18.2
Iowa			
Eldora State Training School for Boys	21.7%	17.1%	27.2%
Woodward Acad.[d]	3.2	1.7	5.9
Kansas			
Judge Riddel Boys Ranch[d]	16.1%	11.5%	22.1%
Kansas Juv. Corr. Complex[c]	15.7	11.3	21.4
Larned Juv. Corr. Fac.	12.0	9.5	15.2
Shawnee Co. Juv. Det. Ctr.[c,d]	12.5	5.8	24.9
Kentucky			
Adair Yth. Dev. Ctr.[c]	12.5%	5.5%	25.9%
Audubon Yth. Dev. Ctr.	5.3	1.6	16.1
Cadet Leadership & Education Program	0.0	0.0	2.4
Green River Yth. Dev. Ctr.	0.0	0.0	2.4
Lake Cumberland Yth. Dev. Ctr.	4.8	1.8	12.0
Lincoln Village Yth. Ctr. & Reg. Juv. Det.[c]	5.6	1.8	16.0
Mayfield Yth. Dev. Ctr.	4.5	1.6	12.1
Morehead Yth. Dev. Ctr.[c]	4.2	1.8	9.5
Northern Kentucky Yth. Dev. Ctr.	3.6	1.5	8.1
Owensboro Trtmt. Ctr.	0.0	0.0	1.6
Louisiana			
Bridge City Ctr. for Yth.	11.6%	7.4%	17.8%
Christian Acres[c,d]	0.0	0.0	8.4
Jetson Corr. Ctr. for Yth.[e]	4.4	1.0	17.9
Swanson Ctr. for Yth.	2.6	0.9	7.8
Ware Yth. Ctr.[c,d]	0.0	0.0	9.7
Maine			
Long Creek Yth. Dev. Ctr.[c]	2.0%	0.7%	5.1%
Mtn. View Yth. Dev. Ctr.	8.6	4.5	16.0
Maryland[f]			
Massachusetts[f]			
Michigan			
Bay Pines Ctr.[c]	20.0%	10.8%	34.1%
W.J. Maxey Boys Training School	11.1	5.8	20.4
Minnesota			
Minnesota Corr. Fac. - Red Wing	4.6%	1.5%	13.1%
Mississippi			
Oakley Yth. Dev. Ctr.[c]	11.9%	7.9%	17.6%

Percent of youth reporting sexual victimization, by facility, National Survey of Youth in Custody, 2012

| | Percent of youth reporting any sexual victimization | | |
| | | 95%-confidence interval | |
Facility name	Weighted percent[a]	Lower bound	Upper bound
Missouri			
Camp Avery	12.5%	9.1%	17.0%
Delmina Woods Yth. Fac.[b]	0.0	0.0	6.3
Ft. Bellefontaine Campus	0.0	0.0	1.5
Fulton Trtmt. Ctr.	10.0	4.7	20.0
Gentry Res. Trtmt. Ctr.	0.0	0.0	5.2
Girardot Ctr. for Yth. & Family	0.0	0.0	4.7
Hillsboro Trtmt. Ctr.	5.3	1.7	14.9
Hogan Street Reg. Yth. Ctr.	8.7	4.4	16.6
Montgomery City Yth. Ctr.[e]	6.3	3.7	10.4
Mount Vernon Trtmt. Ctr.	7.7	4.6	12.7
Northwest Reg. Yth. Ctr.	5.6	1.9	15.4
Rich Hill Yth. Dev. Ctr.	0.0	0.0	3.0
Riverbend Trtmt. Ctr.	4.5	2.0	9.9
Sierra-Osage Trtmt. Ctr.[c]	0.0	0.0	4.6
Spanish Lake Campus	5.3	1.9	13.6
W.E. Sears Yth. Ctr.	7.1	4.4	11.3
Watkins Mill Park Camp[c]	2.2	0.9	5.2
Waverly Reg. Yth. Ctr.	0.0	0.0	2.0
Montana			
Pine Hills Yth. Corr. Fac.	13.0%	5.4%	28.4%
Nebraska			
Yth. Rehab. & Trtmt. Ctr. - Geneva[b]	4.2%	0.9%	17.7%
Nevada			
Caliente Yth. Ctr.[c]	3.3%	0.7%	13.8%
Nevada Yth. Training Ctr.	21.3	10.2	39.4
New Hampshire[f]			
New Jersey			
New Jersey Training School & Intake Fac.	5.3%	1.8%	14.8%
New Mexico			
Camino Nuevo Yth. Ctr.[c]	0.0%	0.0%	3.9%
J. Paul Taylor Ctr.	10.5	3.3	29.0
Yth. Diagnostic & Dev. Ctr. (Males)	0.0	0.0	9.6
New York[f]			
North Carolina			
C.A. Dillon Yth. Dev. Ctr.	5.7%	2.1%	14.8%
Stonewall Jackson Yth. Dev. Ctr.	4.1	1.4	11.0
North Dakota			
North Dakota Yth. Corr. Ctr.[c]	10.8%	6.1%	18.5%
Ohio			
Circleville Juv. Corr. Fac.	30.3%	24.4%	36.9%
Cuyahoga Hills Juv. Corr. Fac.	19.8	14.6	26.2
Indian River Juv. Corr. Fac.	10.5	7.6	14.2
Scioto Juv. Corr. Fac.[c]	23.2	18.1	29.2
Oklahoma[f]			
Oregon			
Camp Florence Yth. Transition Fac.	0.0%	0.0%	3.8%
Camp Tillamook Yth. Transition Fac.	5.6	2.3	12.8
Eastern Oregon Yth. Corr. Fac.	13.3	9.6	18.3
Hillcrest Yth. Corr. Fac.	11.6	9.2	14.6
MacLaren Yth. Corr. Fac.	10.7	7.8	14.4
North Coast Yth. Corr. Fac.	15.8	11.3	21.7
Oak Creek Yth. Corr. Fac.[b]	7.7	4.5	12.8
RiverBend Yth. Transition Fac.	0.0	0.0	3.4
Rogue Valley Yth. Corr. Fac.	13.5	11.0	16.4
Tillamook Yth. Corr. Fac.[e]	11.6	8.4	15.8

Percent of youth reporting sexual victimization, by facility, National Survey of Youth in Custody, 2012

Facility name	Weighted percent[a]	Percent of youth reporting any sexual victimization	
		95%-confidence interval	
		Lower bound	Upper bound
Pennsylvania			
Loysville Yth. Dev. Ctr.	3.3%	0.8%	13.5%
North Central Secure Trtmt.	0.0	0.0	12.8
North Central Secure Trtmt. Unit, Girls Program - Reed Building[b]	0.0	0.0	7.5
Rhode Island			
Thomas C. Slater Training School for Yth.[c]	5.1%	1.9%	12.8%
South Carolina			
AMIkids Beaufort[d]	20.0%	11.6%	32.3%
Birchwood	29.2	20.6	39.5
Camp Aspen	3.6	1.7	7.2
John G. Richards	20.0	14.1	27.6
South Dakota[f]			
Tennessee			
John S. Wilder Yth. Dev. Ctr.	19.5%	9.1%	37.0%
Mountain View Yth. Dev. Ctr.	13.8	5.5	30.6
Taft Yth. Dev. Ctr.	13.0	5.7	27.2
Woodland Hills Yth. Dev. Ctr.	6.7	2.7	15.5
Texas			
Corsicana Res. Trtmt. Ctr.	22.4%	17.1%	28.7%
Evins Reg. Juv. Ctr.	8.6	5.1	14.2
Gainesville State School	15.1	10.6	21.0
Giddings State School	13.3	9.2	19.0
McFadden Ranch	0.0	0.0	4.0
McLennan Co. State Juv. Corr. Fac.	6.1	3.3	10.9
Ron Jackson State Juv. Corr. Complex Unit I[b]	10.8	8.3	14.0
Utah			
Decker Lake Yth. Ctr.	16.7%	8.2%	30.9%
Millcreek Yth. Ctr.[c]	10.7	4.7	22.6
Vermont			
Woodside Juv. Rehab. Ctr.[c]	6.7%	3.1%	13.7%
Virginia			
Beaumont Juv. Corr. Ctr.	15.4%	8.1%	27.3%
Bon Air Juv. Corr. Ctr.[c,e]	4.0	1.1	13.8
Culpeper Juv. Corr. Ctr.[c,e]	13.3	8.5	20.2
Washington			
Green Hill School[e]	7.7%	3.4%	16.6%
Naselle Yth. Camp	1.4	0.3	6.0
West Virginia			
Kenneth Honey Rubenstein Juv. Ctr.	11.1%	7.9%	15.4%
West Virginia Industrial Home for Yth.[c]	14.7	11.8	18.2
Wisconsin			
Copper Lake School[b]	0.0%	0.0%	5.5%
Lincoln Hills School	7.3	4.5	11.7
Mendota Juv. Trtmt. Ctr.	4.8	1.6	13.1
Wyoming			
Wyoming Boys' School	3.0%	0.8%	10.6%
Wyoming Girls' School[b]	0.0	0.0	10.1

Note: Facilities housed males only unless otherwise noted. Facility estimates were listed if they met all of the following criteria: (1) based on at least 15 youth who completed the sexual victimization survey, (2) the facility had a 30% response rate or greater, and (3) the estimates were sufficiently precise to detect a high rate (25% or greater) and had a minimum coefficient of variation of 30%. (See *Methodology* for further discussion of reporting criteria.)

[a]Weighted percentage of youth reporting one or more incidents of sexual victimization involving another youth or facility staff in the past 12 months or since admission to the facility, if less than 12 months.

[b]Facility housed females only.

[c]Facility housed both males and females. Both were sampled at this facility.

[d]Facility was locally or privately operated and held state-placed youth.

[e]Detail may not sum to total because not all youth provided complete data on all types of victimization.

[f]None of the facilities met the criteria for publishing the sexual victimization rate. (See table 5 and appendix tables 6 and 7 for state-level estimates.)

Source: Bureau of Justice Statistics, National Survey of Youth in Custody, 2012.

Percent of youth reporting sexual victimization by another youth, by type of incident and facility, National Survey of Youth in Custody, 2012

	Percent of youth reporting any sexual victimization by another youth[a]					
	All youth-on-youth			Nonconsensual sexual acts		
	Weighted percent	95%-confidence interval		Weighted percent	95%-confidence interval	
Facility name		Lower bound	Upper bound		Lower bound	Upper bound
All facilities - U.S. total	2.5%	2.1%	3.0%	1.7%	1.4%	2.0%
Alabama						
Mt. Meigs Campus	3.2%	1.6%	6.7%	1.8%	0.7%	4.3%
Vacca Campus	7.0	4.1	11.6	4.7	2.4	8.7
Alaska						
McLaughlin Yth. Ctr. Det. & Training[c]	2.7%	1.5%	4.7%	2.7%	1.5%	4.7%
Arizona						
Adobe Mountain School	7.0%	4.0%	12.1%	6.0%	3.2%	10.9%
Black Canyon School[c]	2.0	0.8	4.9	2.0	0.8	4.9
Arkansas						
Arkansas Juv. Assess. & Trtmt. Ctr.[c,d]	11.6%	8.1%	16.4%	8.6%	5.9%	12.4%
Colt Juv. Trtmt. Ctr.	4.8	1.8	11.9	4.8	1.8	11.9
Dermott Juv. Corr. Fac.	3.0	1.2	7.6	3.0	1.2	7.6
Harrisburg Juv. Trtmt. Ctr.	0.0	0.0	3.3	0.0	0.0	3.3
Lewisville Juv. Trtmt. Ctr.[d]	0.0	0.0	4.6	0.0	0.0	4.6
Mansfield Juv. Trtmt. Ctr.	0.0	0.0	3.8	0.0	0.0	3.8
California[e]						
Colorado						
Betty Marler Yth. Srvcs. Ctr.[b,d]	13.8%	9.2%	20.1%	6.9%	3.8%	12.3%
Grand Mesa Yth. Srvcs. Ctr.[c]	0.0	0.0	1.9	0.0	0.0	1.9
Lookout Mtn. Yth. Srvcs. Ctr.	1.7	0.9	3.3	0.9	0.4	2.1
Mt. View Yth. Srvcs. Ctr.[c]	0.0	0.0	3.1	0.0	0.0	3.1
Platte Valley Yth. Srvcs. Ctr.[c]	4.4	2.3	8.4	2.2	0.9	5.5
Ridge View Acad.[d]	2.5	1.2	5.2	1.7	0.7	4.1
Spring Creek Yth. Srvcs. Ctr.[c]	8.7	5.3	14.0	4.5	2.2	9.0
Zebulon Pike Yth. Srvcs. Ctr.	11.5	6.8	19.0	3.8	1.5	9.3
Connecticut[e]						
Delaware						
Ferris School	0.0%	0.0%	8.4%	0.0%	0.0%	8.4%
District of Columbia						
New Beginnings Yth. Dev. Ctr.	0.0%	0.0%	8.5%	0.0%	0.0%	8.5%
Florida						
Bristol Yth. Acad.	0.0%	0.0%	12.5%	0.0%	0.0%	12.5%
Cypress Creek Juv. Offender Corr. Ctr.	0.0	0.0	4.6	0.0	0.0	4.6
Falkenburg Juv. Corr. Fac. - Mental Health	0.0	0.0	7.8	0.0	0.0	7.8
Hastings Comprehensive Mental Health Trtmt. Fac.[d]	3.0	0.7	11.7	3.0	0.7	11.7
Okeechobee Juv. Offender Corr. Ctr.	3.1	0.9	10.0	3.1	0.9	10.0
Okeechobee Yth. Dev. Ctr.[d]	0.0	0.0	7.1	0.0	0.0	7.1
Palm Beach Juv. Corr. Fac.	0.0	0.0	8.8	0.0	0.0	8.8
Palmetto Yth. Acad.	0.0	0.0	8.2	0.0	0.0	8.2
Georgia						
Augusta Reg. Yth. Det. Ctr.	5.0%	1.4%	16.8%	0.0%	0.0%	8.5%
Augusta Yth. Dev. Campus	0.0	0.0	2.0	0.0	0.0	2.0
Crisp Yth. Det. Ctr.	0.0	0.0	10.0	0.0	0.0	10.0
Eastman Yth. Dev. Campus	0.8	0.3	2.2	0.0	0.0	0.9
Gainesville Reg. Yth. Det. Ctr.[c]	6.3	1.8	19.2	0.0	0.0	8.9
Macon Yth. Dev. Campus[b]	2.9	0.9	9.0	2.9	0.9	9.0
Muscogee Yth. Dev. Ctr.	0.0	0.0	2.3	0.0	0.0	2.3
Paulding Reg. Yth. Det. Ctr.	0.0	0.0	6.4	0.0	0.0	6.4
Sumter Yth. Dev. Campus	2.3	1.0	5.3	1.1	0.3	3.7
Hawaii						
Hawaii Yth. Corr. Fac.[c]	5.4%	2.5%	11.2%	5.4%	2.5%	11.2%

Percent of youth reporting sexual victimization by another youth, by type of incident and facility, National Survey of Youth in Custody, 2012

	Percent of youth reporting any sexual victimization by another youth[a]					
	All youth-on-youth			Nonconsensual sexual acts		
		95%-confidence interval			95%-confidence interval	
Facility name	Weighted percent	Lower bound	Upper bound	Weighted percent	Lower bound	Upper bound
Idaho						
Juv. Corr. Ctr. - Lewiston	0.0%	0.0%	2.4%	0.0%	0.0%	2.4%
Juv. Corr. Ctr. - Nampa[c]	1.9	0.7	4.7	0.0	0.0	1.7
Juv. Corr. Ctr. - St. Anthony[c]	1.9	1.1	3.3	1.0	0.5	2.0
Illinois						
Illinois Yth. Ctr. - Chicago	0.0%	0.0%	3.8%	0.0%	0.0%	3.8%
Illinois Yth. Ctr. - Harrisburg	1.0	0.2	3.8	1.0	0.2	3.8
Illinois Yth. Ctr. - Joliet	1.8	0.7	4.2	1.8	0.7	4.2
Illinois Yth. Ctr. - Kewanee	5.4	3.4	8.6	2.6	1.3	5.0
Illinois Yth. Ctr. - St. Charles	0.0	0.0	2.2	0.0	0.0	2.2
Illinois Yth. Ctr. - Warrenville[b]	13.0	6.1	25.6	9.1	3.6	21.2
Indiana						
Camp Summit Boot Camp	0.0%	0.0%	1.1%	0.0%	0.0%	1.1%
Logansport Juv. Corr. Fac/Trtmt. Unit	1.2	0.5	2.6	1.2	0.5	2.6
Madison Juv. Corr. Fac.[b]	8.3	5.2	13.2	2.9	1.2	6.5
Pendleton Juv. Corr. Fac.	1.8	0.8	4.1	0.0	0.0	1.3
South Bend Juv. Corr. Fac.	0.0	0.0	1.2	0.0	0.0	1.2
Iowa						
Eldora State Training School for Boys	2.9%	1.4%	6.0%	1.4%	0.5%	4.0%
Woodward Acad.[d]	1.6	0.7	3.8	0.0	0.0	1.4
Kansas						
Judge Riddel Boys Ranch[d]	3.2%	1.4%	7.1%	3.2%	1.4%	7.1%
Kansas Juv. Corr. Complex[c]	4.1	2.3	7.2	4.1	2.3	7.2
Larned Juv. Corr. Fac.	1.2	0.5	2.7	0.0	0.0	0.8
Shawnee Co. Juv. Det. Ctr.[c,d]	6.3	2.1	16.9	6.3	2.1	16.9
Kentucky						
Adair Yth. Dev. Ctr.[c]	0.0%	0.0%	7.6%	0.0%	0.0%	7.6%
Audubon Yth. Dev. Ctr.	0.0	0.0	7.4	0.0	0.0	7.4
Cadet Leadership & Education Program	0.0	0.0	2.4	0.0	0.0	2.4
Green River Yth. Dev. Ctr.	0.0	0.0	2.4	0.0	0.0	2.4
Lake Cumberland Yth. Dev. Ctr.	0.0	0.0	4.4	0.0	0.0	4.4
Lincoln Village Yth. Dev. Ctr. & Reg. Juv. Det.[c]	0.0	0.0	6.9	0.0	0.0	6.9
Mayfield Yth. Dev. Ctr.	4.5	1.6	12.1	4.5	1.6	12.1
Morehead Yth. Dev. Ctr.[c]	0.0	0.0	3.0	0.0	0.0	3.0
Northern Kentucky Yth. Dev. Ctr.	0.0	0.0	2.6	0.0	0.0	2.6
Owensboro Trtmt. Ctr.	0.0	0.0	1.6	0.0	0.0	1.6
Louisiana						
Bridge City Ctr. for Yth.	0.0%	0.0%	2.6%	0.0%	0.0%	2.6%
Christian Acres[c,d]	0.0	0.0	8.4	0.0	0.0	8.4
Jetson Corr. Ctr. for Yth.	0.0	0.0	9.1	0.0	0.0	9.1
Swanson Ctr. for Yth.	0.0	0.0	8.3	0.0	0.0	8.3
Ware Yth. Ctr.[c,d]	0.0	0.0	9.7	0.0	0.0	9.7
Maine						
Long Creek Yth. Dev. Ctr.[c]	0.0%	0.0%	1.9%	0.0%	0.0%	1.9%
Mtn. View Yth. Dev. Ctr.	5.8	2.6	12.4	5.8	2.6	12.4
Maryland[e]						
Massachusetts[e]						
Michigan						
Bay Pines Ctr.[c]	15.0%	7.3%	28.4%	0.0%	0.0%	7.6%
W.J. Maxey Boys Training School	3.7	1.2	11.1	3.7	1.2	11.1
Minnesota						
Minnesota Corr. Fac. - Red Wing	1.3%	0.3%	4.9%	0.0%	0.0%	4.8%

Percent of youth reporting sexual victimization by another youth, by type of incident and facility, National Survey of Youth in Custody, 2012

	Percent of youth reporting any sexual victimization by another youth[a]					
	All youth-on-youth			Nonconsensual sexual acts		
		95%-confidence interval			95%-confidence interval	
Facility name	Weighted percent	Lower bound	Upper bound	Weighted percent	Lower bound	Upper bound
Mississippi						
Oakley Yth. Dev. Ctr.[c]	4.8%	2.5%	9.0%	0.0%	0.0%	2.1%
Missouri						
Camp Avery	0.0%	0.0%	1.4%	0.0%	0.0%	1.4%
Delmina Woods Yth. Fac.[b]	0.0	0.0	6.3	0.0	0.0	6.3
Ft. Bellefontaine Campus	0.0	0.0	1.5	0.0	0.0	1.5
Fulton Trtmt. Ctr.	10.0	4.7	20.0	5.0	1.8	13.4
Gentry Res. Trtmt. Ctr.	0.0	0.0	5.2	0.0	0.0	5.2
Girardot Ctr. for Yth. & Family	0.0	0.0	4.7	0.0	0.0	4.7
Hillsboro Trtmt. Ctr.	0.0	0.0	6.4	0.0	0.0	6.4
Hogan Street Reg. Yth. Ctr.	0.0	0.0	4.1	0.0	0.0	4.1
Montgomery City Yth. Ctr.	3.1	1.5	6.4	3.1	1.5	6.4
Mount Vernon Trtmt. Ctr.	7.7	4.6	12.7	7.7	4.6	12.7
Northwest Reg. Yth. Ctr.	0.0	0.0	6.3	0.0	0.0	6.3
Rich Hill Yth. Dev.Ctr.	0.0	0.0	3.0	0.0	0.0	3.0
Riverbend Trtmt. Ctr.	0.0	0.0	3.0	0.0	0.0	3.0
Sierra-Osage Trtmt. Ctr.[c]	0.0	0.0	4.6	0.0	0.0	4.6
Spanish Lake Campus	5.3	1.9	13.6	5.3	1.9	13.6
W.E. Sears Yth. Ctr.	2.4	1.0	5.4	2.4	1.0	5.4
Watkins Mill Park Camp[c]	0.0	0.0	1.7	0.0	0.0	1.7
Waverly Reg. Yth. Ctr.	0.0	0.0	2.0	0.0	0.0	2.0
Montana						
Pine Hills Yth. Corr. Fac.	8.7%	2.9%	23.1%	4.5%	1.0%	18.4%
Nebraska						
Yth. Rehab. & Trtmt. Ctr. - Geneva[b]	4.2%	0.9%	17.7%	0.0%	0.0%	10.4%
Nevada						
Caliente Yth. Ctr.[c]	3.3%	0.7%	13.8%	3.3%	0.7%	13.8%
Nevada Yth. Training Ctr.	11.0	3.8	27.6	5.5	1.3	20.9
New Hampshire[e]						
New Jersey						
New Jersey Training School & Intake Fac.	0.0%	0.0%	5.2%	0.0%	0.0%	5.2%
New Mexico						
Camino Nuevo Yth. Ctr.[c]	0.0%	0.0%	3.9%	0.0%	0.0%	3.9%
J. Paul Taylor Ctr.	0.0	0.0	11.6	0.0	0.0	11.6
Yth. Diagnostic & Dev. Ctr. (Males)	0.0	0.0	9.6	0.0	0.0	9.6
New York[e]						
North Carolina						
C.A. Dillon Yth. Dev. Ctr.	0.0%	0.0%	5.8%	0.0%	0.0%	5.8%
Stonewall Jackson Yth. Dev. Ctr.	0.0	0.0	6.7	0.0	0.0	6.7
North Dakota						
North Dakota Yth. Corr. Ctr.[c]	8.1%	4.0%	15.8%	2.7%	1.1%	6.8%
Ohio						
Circleville Juv. Corr. Fac.	3.0%	1.4%	6.4%	3.0%	1.4%	6.4%
Cuyahoga Hills Juv. Corr. Fac.	3.8	1.9	7.3	3.8	1.9	7.3
Indian River Juv. Corr. Fac.	1.9	0.9	3.9	1.0	0.3	2.6
Scioto Juv. Corr. Fac.[c]	5.8	3.2	10.1	5.8	3.2	10.1
Oklahoma[e]						

Percent of youth reporting sexual victimization by another youth, by type of incident and facility, National Survey of Youth in Custody, 2012

	Percent of youth reporting any sexual victimization by another youth[a]					
	All youth-on-youth			Nonconsensual sexual acts		
		95%-confidence interval			95%-confidence interval	
Facility name	Weighted percent	Lower bound	Upper bound	Weighted percent	Lower bound	Upper bound
Oregon						
Camp Florence Yth. Transition Fac.	0.0%	0.0%	3.8%	0.0%	0.0%	3.8%
Camp Tillamook Yth. Transition Fac.	5.6	2.3	12.8	5.6	2.3	12.8
Eastern Oregon Yth. Corr. Fac.	6.7	4.4	9.9	4.4	2.7	7.3
Hillcrest Yth. Corr. Fac.	1.8	1.0	3.3	0.9	0.4	2.2
MacLaren Yth. Corr. Fac.	5.7	3.9	8.4	4.1	2.6	6.6
North Coast Yth. Corr. Fac.	2.6	1.1	6.3	2.6	1.1	6.3
Oak Creek Yth. Corr. Fac.[b]	7.7	4.5	12.8	7.7	4.5	12.8
RiverBend Yth. Transition Fac.	0.0	0.0	3.4	0.0	0.0	3.4
Rogue Valley Yth. Corr. Fac.	3.3	2.2	5.0	2.2	1.3	3.7
Tillamook Yth. Corr. Fac.	7.0	4.6	10.5	7.0	4.6	10.5
Pennsylvania						
Loysville Yth. Dev. Ctr.	0.0%	0.0%	7.8%	0.0%	0.0%	7.8%
North Central Secure Trtmt.	0.0	0.0	12.8	0.0	0.0	12.8
North Central Secure Trtmt. Unit, Girls Program - Reed Building[b]	0.0	0.0	7.5	0.0	0.0	7.5
Rhode Island						
Thomas C. Slater Training School for Yth.[c]	0.0%	0.0%	4.9%	0.0%	0.0%	4.9%
South Carolina						
AMIkids Beaufort[d]	6.7%	2.4%	17.0%	6.7%	2.4%	17.0%
Birchwood	4.0	1.4	10.6	0.0	0.0	4.2
Camp Aspen	0.0	0.0	1.8	0.0	0.0	1.8
John G. Richards	5.0	2.3	10.4	2.5	0.9	7.0
South Dakota[e]						
Tennessee						
John S. Wilder Yth. Dev. Ctr.	0.0%	0.0%	10.0%	0.0%	0.0%	10.0%
Mountain View Yth. Dev. Ctr.	0.0	0.0	10.3	0.0	0.0	10.3
Taft Yth. Dev. Ctr.	0.0	0.0	8.7	0.0	0.0	8.7
Woodland Hills Yth. Dev. Ctr.	0.0	0.0	6.6	0.0	0.0	6.6
Texas						
Corsicana Res. Trtmt. Ctr.	7.9%	5.0%	12.2%	5.3%	3.0%	9.2%
Evins Reg. Juv. Ctr.	0.0	0.0	2.8	0.0	0.0	2.8
Gainesville State School	1.9	0.7	5.3	1.9	0.7	5.3
Giddings State School	0.0	0.0	2.3	0.0	0.0	2.3
McFadden Ranch	0.0	0.0	4.0	0.0	0.0	4.0
McLennan Co. State Juv. Corr. Fac.	1.3	0.3	5.2	1.3	0.3	5.2
Ron Jackson State Juv. Corr. Complex Unit I[b]	6.1	4.2	8.8	4.9	3.2	7.4
Utah						
Decker Lake Yth. Ctr.	5.6%	1.6%	17.2%	5.6%	1.6%	17.2%
Millcreek Yth. Ctr.[c]	3.6	0.9	13.1	3.6	0.9	13.1
Vermont						
Woodside Juv. Rehab. Ctr.[c]	0.0%	0.0%	3.7%	0.0%	0.0%	3.7%
Virginia						
Beaumont Juv. Corr. Ctr.	4.8%	1.3%	16.3%	0.0%	0.0%	5.9%
Bon Air Juv. Corr. Ctr.[c]	0.8	0.2	3.9	0.8	0.2	3.9
Culpeper Juv. Corr. Ctr.[c]	1.7	0.5	5.9	1.7	0.5	5.9
Washington						
Green Hill School	0.9%	0.2%	3.9%	0.9%	0.2%	3.9%
Naselle Yth. Camp	1.4	0.3	6.0	1.4	0.3	6.0
West Virginia						
Kenneth Honey Rubenstein Juv. Ctr.	0.0%	0.0%	1.4%	0.0%	0.0%	1.4%
West Virginia Industrial Home For Yth.[c]	2.6	1.6	4.3	2.6	1.6	4.3

Percent of youth reporting sexual victimization by another youth, by type of incident and facility, National Survey of Youth in Custody, 2012

	Percent of youth reporting any sexual victimization by another youth[a]					
	All youth-on-youth			Nonconsensual sexual acts		
		95%-confidence interval			95%-confidence interval	
Facility name	Weighted percent	Lower bound	Upper bound	Weighted percent	Lower bound	Upper bound
Wisconsin						
Copper Lake School[b]	0.0%	0.0%	5.5%	0.0%	0.0%	5.5%
Lincoln Hills School	0.0	0.0	2.0	0.0	0.0	2.0
Mendota Juv. Trtmt. Ctr.	0.0	0.0	5.4	0.0	0.0	5.4
Wyoming						
Wyoming Boys' School	0.0%	0.0%	5.1%	0.0%	0.0%	5.1%
Wyoming Girls' School[b]	0.0	0.0	10.1	0.0	0.0	10.1

Note: Excludes facilities in which there were no reports of sexual victimization of any type. Facilities housed males only unless otherwise noted. Facility estimates were listed if they met all of the following criteria: (1) based on at least 15 youth who completed the sexual victimization survey, (2) the facility had a 30% response rate or greater, and (3) the estimates were sufficiently precise to detect a high rate (25% or greater) and had a minimum coefficient of variation of 30%. (See *Methodology* for further discussion of reporting criteria.)

[a]Weighted percentage of youth reporting one or more incidents of sexual victimization involving another youth in the past 12 months or since admission to the facility, if less than 12 months.

[b]Facility housed females only.

[c]Facility housed both males and females. Both were sampled at this facility.

[d]Facility was locally or privately operated and held state-placed youth.

[e]None of the facilities met the criteria for publishing the sexual victimization rate. (See table 5 and appendix tables 6 and 7 for state-level estimates.)

Source: Bureau of Justice Statistics, National Survey of Youth in Custody, 2012.

Percent of youth reporting staff sexual misconduct, by type of incident and facility, National Survey of Youth in Custody, 2012

	Percent of youth reporting any staff sexual misconduct[a]					
	All staff sexual misconduct			Sexual acts excluding touching[b]		
		95%-confidence interval			95%-confidence interval	
Facility name	Weighted percent	Lower bound	Upper bound	Weighted percent	Lower bound	Upper bound
All facilities - U.S. total	7.7%	7.0%	8.4%	6.9%	6.3%	7.6%
Alabama						
Mt. Meigs Campus	10.4%	7.0%	15.2%	9.5%	6.2%	14.2%
Vacca Campus	13.6	9.4	19.3	13.6	9.4	19.3
Alaska						
McLaughlin Yth. Ctr. Det. & Training[c]	4.0%	2.5%	6.4%	2.7%	1.5%	4.7%
Arizona						
Adobe Mountain School	3.0%	1.2%	7.2%	2.0%	0.7%	5.8%
Black Canyon School[c]	2.1	0.8	5.0	0.0	0.0	1.7
Arkansas						
Arkansas Juv. Assess. & Trtmt. Ctr.[c,d]	14.2%	10.4%	19.2%	10.2%	7.2%	14.3%
Colt Juv. Trtmt. Ctr.	14.3	8.1	23.9	9.5	4.8	18.1
Dermott Juv. Corr. Fac.	12.1	7.5	18.9	12.1	7.5	18.9
Harrisburg Juv. Trtmt. Ctr.	7.7	4.0	14.2	7.7	4.0	14.2
Lewisville Juv. Trtmt. Ctr.[d]	9.1	4.4	17.9	9.1	4.4	17.9
Mansfield Juv. Trtmt. Ctr.	5.3	2.2	12.0	5.3	2.2	12.0
California[e]						
Colorado						
Betty Marler Yth. Srvcs. Ctr.[b,d]	3.4%	1.4%	8.1%	3.4%	1.4%	8.1%
Grand Mesa Yth. Srvcs. Ctr.[c]	0.0	0.0	1.9	0.0	0.0	1.9
Lookout Mtn. Yth. Srvcs. Ctr.	7.0	4.9	9.8	6.1	4.4	8.5
Mt. View Yth. Srvcs. Ctr.[c]	0.0	0.0	3.1	0.0	0.0	3.1
Platte Valley Yth. Srvcs. Ctr.[c]	4.3	2.2	8.2	2.2	0.9	5.3
Ridge View Acad.[d]	7.9	4.9	12.5	7.9	4.9	12.5
Spring Creek Yth. Srvcs. Ctr.[c]	4.3	2.1	8.6	4.3	2.1	8.6
Zebulon Pike Yth. Srvcs. Ctr.	7.7	4.0	14.3	3.8	1.5	9.3
Connecticut[e]						
Delaware						
Ferris School	0.0%	0.0%	8.4%	0.0%	0.0%	8.4%
District of Columbia						
New Beginnings Yth. Dev. Ctr.	0.0%	0.0%	8.5%	0.0%	0.0%	8.5%
Florida						
Bristol Yth. Acad.	10.7%	3.2%	30.2%	10.7%	3.2%	30.2%
Cypress Creek Juv. Offender Corr. Ctr.	4.7	1.7	12.4	4.7	1.7	12.4
Falkenburg Juv. Corr. Fac. - Mental Health	4.2	1.6	10.8	4.2	1.6	10.8
Hastings Comprehensive Mental Health Trtmt. Prog.[d]	6.0	2.1	15.9	0.0	0.0	6.0
Okeechobee Juv. Offender Corr. Ctr.	7.6	3.6	15.5	4.5	1.7	11.0
Okeechobee Yth. Dev. Ctr.[d]	2.6	0.9	7.6	1.3	0.3	5.6
Palm Beach Juv. Corr. Fac.	16.2	7.3	32.1	16.2	7.3	32.1
Palmetto Yth. Acad.	0.0	0.0	8.2	0.0	0.0	8.2
Georgia						
Augusta Reg. Yth. Det. Ctr.	5.0%	1.4%	16.8%	5.0%	1.4%	16.8%
Augusta Yth. Dev. Campus	20.9	15.8	27.1	19.1	14.1	25.3
Crisp Yth. Det. Ctr.	12.5	5.1	27.5	12.5	5.1	27.5
Eastman Yth. Dev. Campus	23.5	19.8	27.7	21.9	18.2	26.1
Gainesville Reg. Yth. Det. Ctr.[c]	6.3	1.9	19.1	6.3	1.9	19.1
Macon Yth. Dev. Campus[b]	5.1	2.2	11.4	2.9	0.9	9.0
Muscogee Yth. Dev. Ctr.	6.8	3.8	12.0	6.8	3.8	12.0
Paulding Reg. Yth. Det. Ctr.	31.0	20.9	43.4	25.0	15.1	38.5
Sumter Yth. Dev. Campus	18.3	13.5	24.3	17.2	12.5	23.2

Percent of youth reporting staff sexual misconduct, by type of incident and facility, National Survey of Youth in Custody, 2012

	Percent of youth reporting any staff sexual misconduct[a]					
	All staff sexual misconduct			Sexual acts excluding touching[b]		
		95%-confidence interval			95%-confidence interval	
Facility name	Weighted percent	Lower bound	Upper bound	Weighted percent	Lower bound	Upper bound
Hawaii						
Hawaii Yth. Corr. Fac.[c]	5.4%	2.5%	11.2%	5.4%	2.5%	11.2%
Idaho						
Juv. Corr. Ctr. - Lewiston	3.7%	1.7%	8.0%	3.7%	1.7%	8.0%
Juv. Corr. Ctr. - Nampa[c]	1.9	0.7	4.7	1.9	0.7	4.7
Juv. Corr. Ctr. - St. Anthony[c]	1.9	1.1	3.3	1.0	0.5	2.1
Illinois						
Illinois Yth. Ctr. - Chicago	13.5%	8.1%	21.7%	10.8%	6.1%	18.6%
Illinois Yth. Ctr. - Harrisburg	14.7	9.9	21.3	13.9	9.1	20.5
Illinois Yth. Ctr. - Joliet	20.0	15.6	25.2	19.1	15.0	24.1
Illinois Yth. Ctr. - Kewanee	12.0	8.6	16.5	10.3	7.3	14.3
Illinois Yth. Ctr. - St. Charles	5.1	2.7	9.5	5.1	2.7	9.5
Illinois Yth. Ctr. - Warrenville[b]	4.3	1.2	14.5	4.3	1.2	14.5
Indiana						
Camp Summit Boot Camp	2.9%	1.6%	5.2%	2.9%	1.6%	5.2%
Logansport Juv. Corr. Fac./Trtmt. Unit	8.2	6.2	10.9	8.2	6.2	10.9
Madison Juv. Corr. Fac.[b]	0.0	0.0	2.0	0.0	0.0	2.0
Pendleton Juv. Corr. Fac.	11.5	7.9	16.5	8.9	5.8	13.5
South Bend Juv. Corr. Fac.	13.6	10.1	18.2	10.8	7.5	15.2
Iowa						
Eldora State Training School for Boys	18.8%	14.4%	24.2%	17.4%	13.1%	22.8%
Woodward Acad.[d]	1.6	0.7	3.8	1.6	0.7	3.8
Kansas						
Judge Riddel Boys Ranch[d]	12.9%	8.8%	18.5%	12.9%	8.8%	18.5%
Kansas Juv. Corr. Complex[c]	14.9	10.5	20.6	14.0	9.8	19.8
Larned Juv. Corr. Fac.	10.8	8.4	13.9	9.6	7.3	12.6
Shawnee Co. Juv. Det. Ctr.[c,d]	12.5	5.8	24.9	12.5	5.8	24.9
Kentucky						
Adair Yth. Dev. Ctr.[c]	12.5%	5.5%	25.9%	12.5%	5.5%	25.9%
Audubon Yth. Dev. Ctr.	5.3	1.6	16.1	5.3	1.6	16.1
Cadet Leadership & Education Program	0.0	0.0	2.4	0.0	0.0	2.4
Green River Yth. Dev. Ctr.	0.0	0.0	2.4	0.0	0.0	2.4
Lake Cumberland Yth. Dev. Ctr.	4.8	1.8	12.0	4.8	1.8	12.0
Lincoln Village Yth. Dev. Ctr. & Reg. Juv. Det.[c]	5.6	1.8	16.0	5.6	1.8	16.0
Mayfield Yth. Dev. Ctr.	0.0	0.0	4.8	0.0	0.0	4.8
Morehead Yth. Dev. Ctr.[c]	4.2	1.8	9.5	0.0	0.0	3.0
Northern Kentucky Yth. Dev. Ctr.	3.6	1.5	8.1	3.6	1.5	8.1
Owensboro Trtmt. Ctr.	0.0	0.0	1.6	0.0	0.0	1.6
Louisiana						
Bridge City Ctr. for Yth.	11.6%	7.4%	17.8%	10.3%	6.3%	16.3%
Christian Acres[c,d]	0.0	0.0	8.4	0.0	0.0	8.4
Jetson Corr. Ctr. for Yth.	4.3	0.9	17.7	4.3	0.9	17.7
Swanson Ctr. for Yth.	2.6	0.9	7.8	2.6	0.9	7.8
Ware Yth. Ctr.[c,d]	0.0	0.0	9.7	0.0	0.0	9.7
Maine						
Long Creek Yth. Dev. Ctr.[c]	2.0%	0.7%	5.1%	0.0%	0.0%	1.9%
Mtn. View Yth. Dev. Ctr.	5.8	2.6	12.4	5.8	2.6	12.4
Maryland[e]						
Massachusetts[e]						
Michigan						
Bay Pines Ctr.[c]	5.0%	1.5%	15.8%	0.0%	0.0%	7.6%
W.J. Maxey Boys Training School	7.4	3.3	15.8	7.4	3.3	15.8

Percent of youth reporting staff sexual misconduct, by type of incident and facility, National Survey of Youth in Custody, 2012

	Percent of youth reporting any staff sexual misconduct[a]					
	All staff sexual misconduct			Sexual acts excluding touching[b]		
		95%-confidence interval			95%-confidence interval	
Facility name	Weighted percent	Lower bound	Upper bound	Weighted percent	Lower bound	Upper bound
Minnesota						
Minnesota Corr. Fac. - Red Wing	3.3%	0.8%	12.4%	3.3%	0.8%	12.4%
Mississippi						
Oakley Yth. Dev. Ctr.[c]	9.8%	6.1%	15.2%	9.8%	6.1%	15.2%
Missouri						
Camp Avery	12.5%	9.1%	17.0%	8.3%	5.6%	12.2%
Delmina Woods Yth. Fac.[b]	0.0	0.0	6.3	0.0	0.0	6.3
Ft. Bellefontaine Campus	0.0	0.0	1.5	0.0	0.0	1.5
Fulton Trtmt. Ctr.	5.0	1.8	13.4	5.0	1.8	13.4
Gentry Res. Trtmt. Ctr.	0.0	0.0	5.2	0.0	0.0	5.2
Girardot Ctr. for Yth. & Family	0.0	0.0	4.7	0.0	0.0	4.7
Hillsboro Trtmt. Ctr.	5.3	1.7	14.9	5.3	1.7	14.9
Hogan Street Reg. Yth. Ctr.	8.7	4.4	16.6	8.7	4.4	16.6
Montgomery City Yth. Ctr.	3.1	1.5	6.4	3.1	1.5	6.4
Mount Vernon Trtmt. Ctr.	0.0	0.0	2.1	0.0	0.0	2.1
Northwest Reg. Yth. Ctr.	5.6	1.9	15.4	5.6	1.9	15.4
Rich Hill Yth. Dev. Ctr.	0.0	0.0	3.0	0.0	0.0	3.0
Riverbend Trtmt. Ctr.	4.5	2.0	9.9	4.5	2.0	9.9
Sierra-Osage Trtmt. Ctr.[c]	0.0	0.0	4.6	0.0	0.0	4.6
Spanish Lake Campus	0.0	0.0	5.2	0.0	0.0	5.2
W.E. Sears Yth. Ctr.	4.8	2.6	8.4	4.8	2.6	8.4
Watkins Mill Park Camp[c]	2.2	0.9	5.2	0.0	0.0	1.7
Waverly Reg. Yth. Ctr.	0.0	0.0	2.0	0.0	0.0	2.0
Montana						
Pine Hills Yth. Corr. Fac.	8.7%	2.9%	23.1%	8.7%	2.9%	23.1%
Nebraska						
Yth. Rehab. & Trtmt. Ctr. - Geneva[b]	0.0%	0.0%	10.4%	0.0%	0.0%	10.4%
Nevada						
Caliente Yth. Ctr.[c]	3.3%	0.7%	13.8%	3.3%	0.7%	13.8%
Nevada Yth. Training Ctr.	15.9	7.3	31.0	15.9	7.3	31.0
New Hampshire[e]						
New Jersey						
New Jersey Training School & Intake Fac.	5.3%	1.8%	14.8%	5.3%	1.8%	14.8%
New Mexico						
Camino Nuevo Yth. Ctr. [c]	0.0%	0.0%	3.9%	0.0%	0.0%	3.9%
J. Paul Taylor Ctr.	10.5	3.3	29.0	10.5	3.3	29.0
Yth. Diagnostic & Dev. Ctr. (Males)	0.0	0.0	9.6	0.0	0.0	9.6
New York[e]						
North Carolina						
C.A. Dillon Yth. Dev. Ctr.	5.7%	2.1%	14.8%	5.7%	2.1%	14.8%
Stonewall Jackson Yth. Dev. Ctr.	4.1	1.4	11.0	4.1	1.4	11.0
North Dakota						
North Dakota Yth. Corr. Ctr.[c]	2.7%	1.1%	6.8%	0.0%	0.0%	2.5%
Ohio						
Circleville Juv. Corr. Fac.	28.8%	22.9%	35.5%	27.3%	21.4%	34.0%
Cuyahoga Hills Juv. Corr. Fac.	16.0	11.0	22.7	15.1	10.4	21.3
Indian River Juv. Corr. Fac.	9.5	6.8	13.2	9.5	6.8	13.2
Scioto Juv. Corr. Fac.[c]	18.8	14.0	24.9	14.7	10.4	20.4
Oklahoma[e]						

Percent of youth reporting staff sexual misconduct, by type of incident and facility, National Survey of Youth in Custody, 2012

Facility name	Percent of youth reporting any staff sexual misconduct[a]					
	All staff sexual misconduct			Sexual acts excluding touching[b]		
	Weighted percent	95%-confidence interval		Weighted percent	95%-confidence interval	
		Lower bound	Upper bound		Lower bound	Upper bound
Oregon						
Camp Florence Yth. Transition Fac.	0.0%	0.0%	3.8%	0.0%	0.0%	3.8%
Camp Tillamook Yth. Transition Fac.	0.0	0.0	4.2	0.0	0.0	4.2
Eastern Oregon Yth. Corr. Fac.	6.7	4.4	9.9	2.2	1.1	4.5
Hillcrest Yth. Corr. Fac.	10.5	8.2	13.4	10.5	8.2	13.4
MacLaren Yth. Corr. Fac.	7.4	5.1	10.6	6.6	4.4	9.8
North Coast Yth. Corr. Fac.	13.2	8.9	18.9	13.2	8.9	18.9
Oak Creek Yth. Corr. Fac.[b]	0.0	0.0	2.2	0.0	0.0	2.2
RiverBend Yth. Transition Fac.	0.0	0.0	3.4	0.0	0.0	3.4
Rogue Valley Yth. Corr. Fac.	12.4	9.9	15.3	11.2	8.9	14.1
Tillamook Yth. Corr. Fac.	4.5	2.7	7.5	4.5	2.7	7.5
Pennsylvania						
Loysville Yth. Dev. Ctr.	3.3%	0.8%	13.5%	3.3%	0.8%	13.5%
North Central Secure Trtmt.	0.0	0.0	12.8	0.0	0.0	12.8
North Central Secure Trtmt. Unit, Girls Program - Reed Building[b]	0.0	0.0	7.5	0.0	0.0	7.5
Rhode Island						
Thomas C. Slater Training School for Yth.[c]	5.1%	1.9%	12.8%	2.0%	0.5%	7.1%
South Carolina						
AMikids Beaufort[d]	20.0%	11.6%	32.3%	14.3%	7.2%	26.2%
Birchwood	29.2	20.6	39.5	26.1	17.5	37.0
Camp Aspen	3.6	1.7	7.2	3.6	1.7	7.2
John G. Richards	15.0	9.9	22.0	15.0	9.9	22.0
South Dakota[e]						
Tennessee						
John S. Wilder Yth. Dev. Ctr.	19.5%	9.1%	37.0%	19.5%	9.1%	37.0%
Mountain View Yth. Dev. Ctr.	13.8	5.5	30.6	13.8	5.5	30.6
Taft Yth. Dev. Ctr.	13.0	5.7	27.2	13.0	5.7	27.2
Woodland Hills Yth. Dev. Ctr.	6.7	2.7	15.5	6.7	2.7	15.5
Texas						
Corsicana Res. Trtmt. Ctr.	18.4%	13.4%	24.8%	18.4%	13.4%	24.8%
Evins Reg. Juv. Ctr.	8.6	5.1	14.2	8.6	5.1	14.2
Gainesville State School	13.2	8.9	19.1	13.2	8.9	19.1
Giddings State School	13.3	9.2	19.0	9.6	6.0	15.0
McFadden Ranch	0.0	0.0	4.0	0.0	0.0	4.0
McLennan Co. State Juv. Corr. Fac.	4.8	2.5	9.1	4.8	2.5	9.1
Ron Jackson State Juv. Corr. Complex Unit I[b]	8.3	6.1	11.2	6.0	4.2	8.7
Utah						
Decker Lake Yth. Ctr.	11.1%	4.6%	24.4%	0.0%	0.0%	8.1%
Millcreek Yth. Ctr.[c]	10.7	4.7	22.6	10.7	4.7	22.6
Vermont						
Woodside Juv. Rehab. Ctr.[c]	6.7%	3.1%	13.7%	6.7%	3.1%	13.7%
Virginia						
Beaumont Juv. Corr. Ctr.	10.6%	5.2%	20.4%	6.7%	3.7%	12.0%
Bon Air Juv. Corr. Ctr.[c]	3.1	0.7	13.8	3.1	0.7	13.8
Culpeper Juv. Corr. Ctr.[c]	11.5	7.1	18.0	10.0	5.9	16.5
Washington						
Green Hill School	6.7%	2.7%	15.6%	6.7%	2.7%	15.6%
Naselle Yth. Camp	0.0	0.0	9.9	0.0	0.0	9.9
West Virginia						
Kenneth Honey Rubenstein Juv. Ctr.	11.1%	7.9%	15.4%	11.1%	7.9%	15.4%
West Virginia Industrial Home for Yth.[c]	13.4	10.6	16.8	12.1	9.6	15.1

Percent of youth reporting staff sexual misconduct, by type of incident and facility, National Survey of Youth in Custody, 2012

	Percent of youth reporting any staff sexual misconduct[a]					
	All staff sexual misconduct			Sexual acts excluding touching[b]		
		95%-confidence interval			95%-confidence interval	
Facility name	Weighted percent	Lower bound	Upper bound	Weighted percent	Lower bound	Upper bound
Wisconsin						
Copper Lake School[b]	0.0%	0.0%	5.5%	0.0%	0.0%	5.5%
Lincoln Hills School	7.3	4.5	11.7	7.3	4.5	11.7
Mendota Juv. Trtmt. Ctr.	4.8	1.6	13.1	4.8	1.6	13.1
Wyoming						
Wyoming Boys' School	3.0%	0.8%	10.6%	3.0%	0.8%	10.6%
Wyoming Girls' School[b]	0.0	0.0	10.1	0.0	0.0	10.1

Note: Excludes facilities in which there were no reports of sexual victimization of any type. Facilities housed males only unless otherwise noted. Facility estimates were listed if they met all of the following criteria: (1) based on at least 15 youth who completed the sexual victimization survey, (2) the facility had a 30% response rate or greater, and (3) the estimates were sufficiently precise to detect a high rate (25% or greater) and had a minimum coefficient of variation of 30%. (See *Methodology* for further discussion of reporting criteria.)

[a]Weighted percentage of youth reporting one or more incidents of sexual victimization involving facility staff in the past 12 months or since admission to the facility, if less than 12 months.

[b]Facility housed females only.

[c]Facility housed both males and females . Both were sampled at this facility.

[d]Facility was locally or privately operated and held state-placed youth.

[e]None of the facilities met the criteria for publishing the sexual victimization rate. (See table 5 and appendix tables 6 and 7 for state-level estimates.)

Source: Bureau of Justice Statistics, National Survey of Youth in Custody, 2012.

Percent of youth reporting staff sexual misconduct excluding touching, by use of force and facility, National Survey of Youth in Custody, 2012

	Percent of youth reporting any staff sexual misconduct excluding touching[a]					
	Force reported			No report of force		
		95%-confidence interval			95%-confidence interval	
Facility name	Weighted percent	Lower bound	Upper bound	Weighted percent	Lower bound	Upper bound
All facilities - U.S. total	3.1%	2.7%	3.5%	4.3%	3.7%	4.9%
Alabama						
Mt. Meigs Campus	4.4%	2.2%	8.7%	3.8%	2.0%	6.9%
Vacca Campus	4.5	2.4	8.5	9.3	5.9	14.4
Alaska						
McLaughlin Yth. Ctr. Det. & Training[c]	1.3%	0.6%	3.0%	1.3%	0.6%	3.0%
Arizona						
Adobe Mountain School	0.0%	0.0%	2.5%	2.0%	0.7%	5.8%
Black Canyon School[c]	0.0	0.0	1.7	0.0	0.0	1.7
Arkansas						
Arkansas Juv. Assess. & Trtmt. Ctr.[c,d]	2.7%	1.4%	5.4%	8.9%	6.1%	12.8%
Colt Juv. Trtmt. Ctr.	9.5	4.8	18.1	0.0	0.0	4.4
Dermott Juv. Corr. Fac.	3.0	1.2	7.6	9.1	5.2	15.3
Harrisburg Juv. Trtmt. Ctr.	7.7	4.0	14.2	3.8	1.5	9.4
Lewisville Juv. Trtmt. Ctr.[d]	4.5	1.7	11.8	4.5	1.7	11.8
Mansfield Juv. Trtmt. Ctr.	5.3	2.2	12.0	0.0	0.0	3.8
California[e]						
Colorado						
Betty Marler Yth. Srvcs. Ctr.[b,d]	3.4%	1.4%	8.1%	0.0%	0.0%	2.7%
Grand Mesa Yth. Srvcs. Ctr.[c]	0.0	0.0	1.9	0.0	0.0	1.9
Lookout Mtn. Yth. Srvcs. Ctr.	1.7	0.9	3.3	4.4	2.9	6.5
Mt. View Yth. Srvcs. Ctr.[c]	0.0	0.0	3.1	0.0	0.0	3.1
Platte Valley Yth. Srvcs. Ctr.[c]	2.2	0.9	5.3	0.0	0.0	1.9
Ridge View Acad.[d]	3.7	1.7	7.9	4.2	2.3	7.5
Spring Creek Yth. Srvcs. Ctr.[c]	0.0	0.0	2.7	4.3	2.1	8.6
Zebulon Pike Yth. Srvcs. Ctr.	3.8	1.5	9.3	0.0	0.0	3.3
Connecticut[e]						
Delaware						
Ferris School	0.0%	0.0%	8.4%	0.0%	0.0%	8.4%
District of Columbia						
New Beginnings Yth. Dev. Ctr.	0.0%	0.0%	8.5%	0.0%	0.0%	8.5%
Florida						
Bristol Yth. Acad.	7.8%	1.7%	28.9%	2.9%	0.7%	11.5%
Cypress Creek Juv. Offender Corr. Ctr.	3.3	0.9	11.6	1.4	0.4	5.2
Falkenburg Juv. Corr. Fac. - Mental Health	2.1	0.6	7.8	2.1	0.6	7.8
Hastings Comprehensive Mental Health Trtmt. Prog.[d]	0.0	0.0	6.0	0.0	0.0	6.0
Okeechobee Juv. Offender Corr. Ctr.	1.4	0.4	4.5	3.1	0.9	10.0
Okeechobee Yth. Dev. Ctr.[d]	0.0	0.0	7.1	1.3	0.3	5.6
Palm Beach Juv. Corr. Fac.	13.5	5.4	30.0	2.7	0.9	7.7
Palmetto Yth. Acad.	0.0	0.0	8.2	0.0	0.0	8.2
Georgia						
Augusta Reg. Yth. Det. Ctr.	0.0%	0.0%	8.5%	5.0%	1.4%	16.8%
Augusta Yth. Dev. Campus	11.8	7.8	17.3	5.6	3.1	9.7
Crisp Yth. Det. Ctr.	12.5	5.1	27.5	0.0	0.0	10.0
Eastman Yth. Dev. Campus	12.3	9.4	16.0	10.6	7.9	14.1
Gainesville Reg. Yth. Det. Ctr.[c]	6.3	1.9	19.1	0.0	0.0	8.9
Macon Yth. Dev. Campus[b]	2.9	0.9	9.0	0.0	0.0	3.9
Muscogee Yth. Dev. Ctr.	2.8	1.0	7.3	2.1	0.8	5.5
Paulding Reg. Yth. Det. Ctr.	7.1	2.7	17.6	22.2	12.8	35.7
Sumter Yth. Dev. Campus	10.3	7.0	15.0	8.1	5.1	12.5
Hawaii						
Hawaii Yth. Corr. Fac.[c]	0.0%	0.0%	3.2%	2.8%	1.0%	7.8%

Percent of youth reporting staff sexual misconduct excluding touching, by use of force and facility, National Survey of Youth in Custody, 2012

	Percent of youth reporting any staff sexual misconduct excluding touching[a]					
	Force reported			No report of force		
		95%-confidence interval			95%-confidence interval	
Facility name	Weighted percent	Lower bound	Upper bound	Weighted percent	Lower bound	Upper bound
Idaho						
Juv. Corr. Ctr. - Lewiston	0.0%	0.0%	2.4%	3.7%	1.7%	8.0%
Juv. Corr. Ctr. - Nampa[c]	0.0	0.0	1.7	1.9	0.7	4.7
Juv. Corr. Ctr. - St. Anthony[c]	0.0	0.0	0.6	1.0	0.5	2.1
Illinois						
Illinois Yth. Ctr. - Chicago	5.4%	2.4%	11.9%	8.1%	4.1%	15.5%
Illinois Yth. Ctr. - Harrisburg	4.9	2.6	9.0	8.9	5.7	13.6
Illinois Yth. Ctr. - Joliet	12.4	9.0	16.8	6.2	3.9	9.6
Illinois Yth. Ctr. - Kewanee	4.3	2.6	7.1	6.0	3.9	9.1
Illinois Yth. Ctr. - St. Charles	1.7	0.6	4.9	5.1	2.7	9.5
Illinois Yth. Ctr. - Warrenville[b]	0.0	0.0	7.2	4.3	1.2	14.5
Indiana						
Camp Summit Boot Camp	1.4%	0.6%	3.3%	1.4%	0.6%	3.3%
Logansport Juv. Corr. Fac./Trtmt. Unit	4.7	3.2	6.9	4.7	3.2	7.0
Madison Juv. Corr. Fac.[b]	0.0	0.0	2.0	0.0	0.0	2.0
Pendleton Juv. Corr. Fac.	3.6	1.7	7.2	5.5	3.4	8.7
South Bend Juv. Corr. Fac.	6.1	3.6	10.1	4.6	2.8	7.5
Iowa						
Eldora State Training School for Boys	5.8%	3.5%	9.5%	11.6%	8.3%	16.0%
Woodward Acad.[d]	0.0	0.0	1.4	0.8	0.2	2.7
Kansas						
Judge Riddel Boys Ranch[d]	3.2%	1.4%	7.1%	9.7%	6.2%	14.8%
Kansas Juv. Corr. Complex[c]	9.1	6.2	13.1	9.9	6.1	15.7
Larned Juv. Corr. Fac.	3.6	2.3	5.7	6.0	4.2	8.6
Shawnee Co. Juv. Det. Ctr.[c,d]	0.0	0.0	6.9	12.5	5.8	24.9
Kentucky						
Adair Yth. Dev. Ctr.[c]	6.3%	2.0%	17.8%	6.3%	2.0%	17.8%
Audubon Yth. Dev. Ctr.	5.3	1.6	16.1	5.3	1.6	16.1
Cadet Leadership & Education Program	0.0	0.0	2.4	0.0	0.0	2.4
Green River Yth. Dev. Ctr.	0.0	0.0	2.4	0.0	0.0	2.4
Lake Cumberland Yth. Dev. Ctr.	4.8	1.8	12.0	0.0	0.0	4.4
Lincoln Village Yth. Dev. Ctr. & Reg. Juv. Det.[c]	0.0	0.0	6.9	5.6	1.8	16.0
Mayfield Yth. Dev. Ctr.	0.0	0.0	4.8	0.0	0.0	4.8
Morehead Yth. Dev. Ctr.[c]	0.0	0.0	3.0	0.0	0.0	3.0
Northern Kentucky Yth. Dev. Ctr.	0.0	0.0	2.6	0.0	0.0	2.6
Owensboro Trtmt. Ctr.	0.0	0.0	1.6	0.0	0.0	1.6
Louisiana						
Bridge City Ctr. for Yth.	2.9%	1.1%	7.2%	7.4%	4.1%	12.8%
Christian Acres[c,d]	0.0	0.0	8.4	0.0	0.0	8.4
Jetson Corr. Ctr. for Yth.	0.0	0.0	9.1	4.4	1.0	17.9
Swanson Ctr. for Yth.	0.0	0.0	8.3	2.6	0.9	7.8
Ware Yth. Ctr.[c,d]	0.0	0.0	9.7	0.0	0.0	9.7
Maine						
Long Creek Yth. Dev. Ctr.[c]	0.0%	0.0%	1.9%	0.0%	0.0%	1.9%
Mtn. View Yth. Dev. Ctr.	2.9	0.9	8.5	2.9	0.9	8.5
Maryland[e]						
Massachusetts[e]						
Michigan						
Bay Pines Ctr.[c]	0.0%	0.0%	7.6%	0.0%	0.0%	7.6%
W.J. Maxey Boys Training School	0.0	0.0	6.8	7.4	3.3	15.8
Minnesota						
Minnesota Corr. Fac. - Red Wing	0.0%	0.0%	4.8%	3.3%	0.8%	12.4%

Percent of youth reporting staff sexual misconduct excluding touching, by use of force and facility, National Survey of Youth in Custody, 2012

	Percent of youth reporting any staff sexual misconduct excluding touching[a]					
	Force reported			No report of force		
		95%-confidence interval			95%-confidence interval	
Facility name	Weighted percent	Lower bound	Upper bound	Weighted percent	Lower bound	Upper bound
Mississippi						
Oakley Yth. Dev. Ctr.[c]	2.4%	1.0%	6.0%	7.3%	4.3%	12.3%
Missouri						
Camp Avery	0.0%	0.0%	1.4%	8.3%	5.6%	12.2%
Delmina Woods Yth. Fac.[b]	0.0	0.0	6.3	0.0	0.0	6.3
Ft. Bellefontaine Campus	0.0	0.0	1.5	0.0	0.0	1.5
Fulton Trtmt. Ctr.	5.0	1.8	13.4	0.0	0.0	5.3
Gentry Res. Trtmt. Ctr.	0.0	0.0	5.2	0.0	0.0	5.2
Girardot Ctr. for Yth. & Family	0.0	0.0	4.7	0.0	0.0	4.7
Hillsboro Trtmt. Ctr.	5.3	1.7	14.9	0.0	0.0	6.4
Hogan Street Reg. Yth. Ctr.	4.3	1.7	10.9	4.3	1.7	10.9
Montgomery City Yth. Ctr.	0.0	0.0	1.7	3.1	1.5	6.4
Mount Vernon Trtmt. Ctr.	0.0	0.0	2.1	0.0	0.0	2.1
Northwest Reg. Yth. Ctr.	5.6	1.9	15.4	0.0	0.0	6.3
Rich Hill Yth. Dev.Ctr.	0.0	0.0	3.0	0.0	0.0	3.0
Riverbend Trtmt. Ctr.	4.5	2.0	9.9	0.0	0.0	3.0
Sierra-Osage Trtmt. Ctr.[c]	0.0	0.0	4.6	0.0	0.0	4.6
Spanish Lake Campus	0.0	0.0	5.2	0.0	0.0	5.2
W.E. Sears Yth. Ctr.	0.0	0.0	1.7	2.4	1.1	5.5
Watkins Mill Park Camp[c]	0.0	0.0	1.7	0.0	0.0	1.7
Waverly Reg. Yth. Ctr.	0.0	0.0	2.0	0.0	0.0	2.0
Montana						
Pine Hills Yth. Corr. Fac.	4.3%	1.0%	17.6%	4.3%	1.0%	17.7%
Nebraska						
Yth. Rehab. & Trtmt. Ctr. - Geneva[b]	0.0%	0.0%	10.4%	0.0%	0.0%	10.4%
Nevada						
Caliente Yth. Ctr.[c]	3.3%	0.7%	13.8%	0.0%	0.0%	7.1%
Nevada Yth. Training Ctr.	14.2	6.1	29.7	3.3	1.2	8.8
New Hampshire[e]						
New Jersey						
New Jersey Training School & Intake Fac.	3.5%	0.8%	14.4%	5.3%	1.8%	14.8%
New Mexico						
Camino Nuevo Yth. Ctr.[c]	0.0%	0.0%	3.9%	0.0%	0.0%	3.9%
J. Paul Taylor Ctr.	7.4	1.6	27.5	3.2	0.8	12.3
Yth. Diagnostic & Dev. Ctr. (Males)	0.0	0.0	9.6	0.0	0.0	9.6
New York[e]						
North Carolina						
C.A. Dillon Yth. Dev. Ctr.	2.9%	0.7%	10.7%	5.7%	2.1%	14.8%
Stonewall Jackson Yth. Dev. Ctr.	2.0	0.5	8.2	4.1	1.4	11.0
North Dakota						
North Dakota Yth. Corr. Ctr.[c]	0.0%	0.0%	2.5%	0.0%	0.0%	2.5%
Ohio						
Circleville Juv. Corr. Fac.	15.2%	10.6%	21.1%	15.2%	10.6%	21.1%
Cuyahoga Hills Juv. Corr. Fac.	2.6	1.0	6.7	12.5	8.6	17.7
Indian River Juv. Corr. Fac.	0.0	0.0	1.0	8.7	6.3	11.8
Scioto Juv. Corr. Fac.[c]	9.0	5.6	14.1	4.5	2.3	8.7
Oklahoma[e]						

Percent of youth reporting staff sexual misconduct excluding touching, by use of force and facility, National Survey of Youth in Custody, 2012

	Percent of youth reporting any staff sexual misconduct excluding touching[a]					
	Force reported			No report of force		
		95%-confidence interval			95%-confidence interval	
Facility name	Weighted percent	Lower bound	Upper bound	Weighted percent	Lower bound	Upper bound
Oregon						
Camp Florence Yth. Transition Fac.	0.0%	0.0%	3.8%	0.0%	0.0%	3.8%
Camp Tillamook Yth. Transition Fac.	0.0	0.0	4.2	0.0	0.0	4.2
Eastern Oregon Yth. Corr. Fac.	0.0	0.0	1.2	2.2	1.1	4.5
Hillcrest Yth. Corr. Fac.	3.6	2.1	6.1	6.3	4.6	8.6
MacLaren Yth. Corr. Fac.	2.5	1.3	4.5	4.1	2.3	7.1
North Coast Yth. Corr. Fac.	5.3	2.8	9.7	7.9	4.7	13.0
Oak Creek Yth. Corr. Fac.[b]	0.0	0.0	2.2	0.0	0.0	2.2
RiverBend Yth. Transition Fac.	0.0	0.0	3.4	0.0	0.0	3.4
Rogue Valley Yth. Corr. Fac.	4.5	3.1	6.4	7.9	6.0	10.2
Tillamook Yth. Corr. Fac.	0.0	0.0	1.2	4.7	2.8	7.7
Pennsylvania						
Loysville Yth. Dev. Ctr.	0.0%	0.0%	7.8%	3.3%	0.8%	13.5%
North Central Secure Trtmt.	0.0	0.0	12.8	0.0	0.0	12.8
North Central Secure Trtmt. Unit, Girls Program - Reed Building[b]	0.0	0.0	7.5	0.0	0.0	7.5
Rhode Island						
Thomas C. Slater Training School for Yth.[c]	0.0%	0.0%	4.9%	2.0%	0.5%	7.1%
South Carolina						
AMIkids Beaufort[d]	6.7%	2.4%	17.0%	7.1%	2.6%	18.3%
Birchwood	18.2	11.0	28.6	4.5	1.6	12.1
Camp Aspen	3.6	1.7	7.2	0.0	0.0	1.8
John G. Richards	5.0	2.3	10.4	10.0	6.0	16.3
South Dakota[e]						
Tennessee						
John S. Wilder Yth. Dev. Ctr.	6.5%	1.8%	21.2%	13.0%	5.0%	29.7%
Mountain View Yth. Dev.Ctr.	1.4	0.3	6.2	12.4	4.6	29.6
Taft Yth. Dev. Ctr.	4.3	1.1	16.0	8.7	3.1	21.9
Woodland Hills Yth. Dev. Ctr.	1.1	0.3	4.8	5.6	2.0	14.5
Texas						
Corsicana Res. Trtmt. Ctr.	9.3%	5.8%	14.8%	10.7%	7.2%	15.6%
Evins Reg. Juv. Ctr.	4.3	2.0	9.1	4.3	2.0	9.0
Gainesville State School	6.6	3.8	11.2	7.5	4.2	13.2
Giddings State School	5.8	2.9	11.2	5.8	3.3	10.0
McFadden Ranch	0.0	0.0	4.0	0.0	0.0	4.0
McLennan Co. State Juv. Corr. Fac.	1.8	0.7	5.0	3.9	1.8	8.1
Ron Jackson State Juv. Corr. Complex Unit I[b]	3.7	2.3	5.9	1.2	0.5	2.8
Utah						
Decker Lake Yth. Ctr.	0.0%	0.0%	8.1%	0.0%	0.0%	8.1%
Millcreek Yth. Ctr.[c]	3.6	0.9	13.1	7.1	2.6	18.0
Vermont						
Woodside Juv. Rehab. Ctr.[c]	0.0%	0.0%	3.7%	6.7%	3.1%	13.7%
Virginia						
Beaumont Juv. Corr. Ctr.	1.0%	0.2%	4.3%	4.9%	2.4%	9.7%
Bon Air Juv. Corr. Ctr.[c]	0.0	0.0	7.4	3.1	0.7	13.8
Culpeper Juv. Corr. Ctr.[c]	4.9	2.3	10.2	6.8	3.5	12.7
Washington						
Green Hill School	2.6%	0.6%	10.6%	0.9%	0.2%	3.9%
Naselle Yth. Camp	0.0	0.0	9.9	0.0	0.0	9.9
West Virginia						
Kenneth Honey Rubenstein Juv. Ctr.	2.8%	1.4%	5.5%	8.3%	5.6%	12.3%
West Virginia Industrial Home for Yth.[c]	2.6	1.6	4.3	9.5	7.2	12.2

Percent of youth reporting staff sexual misconduct excluding touching, by use of force and facility, National Survey of Youth in Custody, 2012

	Percent of youth reporting any staff sexual misconduct excluding touching[a]					
	Force reported			No report of force		
		95%-confidence interval			95%-confidence interval	
Facility name	Weighted percent	Lower bound	Upper bound	Weighted percent	Lower bound	Upper bound
Wisconsin						
Copper Lake School[b]	0.0%	0.0%	5.5%	0.0%	0.0%	5.5%
Lincoln Hills School	2.7	1.2	6.1	5.5	3.1	9.5
Mendota Juv. Trtmt. Ctr.	0.0	0.0	5.4	4.8	1.6	13.1
Wyoming						
Wyoming Boys' School	0.0%	0.0%	5.1%	3.0%	0.8%	10.6%
Wyoming Girls' School[b]	0.0	0.0	10.1	0.0	0.0	10.1

Note: Excludes facilities in which there were no reports of sexual victimization of any type. Facilities housed males only unless otherwise noted. Facility estimates were listed if they met all of the following criteria: (1) based on at least 15 youth who completed the sexual victimization survey, (2) the facility had a 30% response rate or greater, and (3) the estimates were sufficiently precise to detect a high rate (25% or greater) and had a minimum coefficient of variation of 30%. (See *Methodology* for further discussion of reporting criteria.)

[a]Weighted percentage of youth reporting one or more incidents of sexual victimization involving facility staff in the past 12 months or since admission to the facility, if less than 12 months.

[b]Facility housed females only.

[c]Facility housed both males and females. Both were sampled at this facility.

[d]Facility was locally or privately operated and held state-placed youth.

[e]None of the facilities met the criteria for publishing the sexual victimization rate. (See table 5 and appendix tables 6 and 7 for state-level estimates.)

Source: Bureau of Justice Statistics, National Survey of Youth in Custody, 2012.

APPENDIX TABLE 6
Characteristics of juvenile facilities used to provide state-level estimates, National Survey of Youth in Custody, 2012

State[b]	Number of facilities[c]	Number of sampled youth	Number of ineligible youth[d]	Number of respondents[a] All completed NSYC-2 interviews	Sexual victimization survey	Response rate[e]
Total[e]	312	15,969	6,124	9,565	8,579	59.9%
Alabama	2	204	29	146	132	71.6
Alaska	3	123	23	112	101	91.1
Arizona	2	222	239	165	149	74.3
Arkansas	10	301	179	255	230	84.7
California	4	792	227	190	167	24.0
Colorado	8	562	155	473	424	84.2
Delaware	1	39	3	24	21	61.5
District of Columbia	1	46	15	27	24	58.7
Florida	36	1,644	312	636	573	38.7
Georgia	17	806	1,189	552	497	68.5
Hawaii	1	53	7	42	37	79.2
Idaho	3	223	38	206	184	92.4
Illinois	6	679	501	505	451	74.4
Indiana	5	474	118	414	370	87.3
Iowa	4	284	82	239	214	84.2
Kansas	4	317	173	282	252	89.0
Kentucky	13	281	76	246	222	87.5
Louisiana	10	587	145	250	226	42.6
Maine	2	126	17	101	90	80.2
Maryland	8	291	185	58	51	19.9
Massachusetts	16	160	70	95	87	59.4
Michigan	4	152	34	66	60	43.4
Minnesota	3	143	42	66	61	46.2
Mississippi	1	54	0	47	42	87.0
Missouri	28	637	83	576	517	90.4
Montana	1	64	13	25	23	39.1
Nebraska	1	78	23	27	24	34.6
Nevada	2	195	37	84	75	43.1
New Jersey	12	416	264	195	174	46.9
New Mexico	3	202	43	103	95	51.0
New York	9	460	112	57	51	12.4
North Carolina	6	268	55	117	105	43.7
North Dakota	3	71	35	60	54	84.5
Ohio	4	495	146	370	329	74.7
Oklahoma	6	188	45	53	46	28.2
Oregon	10	712	81	628	561	88.2
Pennsylvania	9	320	91	156	139	48.8
Rhode Island	1	74	39	43	39	58.1
South Carolina	4	142	30	122	108	85.9
South Dakota	6	138	54	53	45	38.4
Tennessee	4	362	107	152	134	42.0
Texas	12	957	491	701	633	73.2
Utah	8	211	65	113	100	53.6
Vermont	1	17	5	16	15	94.1
Virginia	3	478	99	189	174	39.5
Washington	8	470	162	180	160	38.3
West Virginia	2	125	4	121	109	96.8
Wisconsin	3	216	154	165	148	76.4
Wyoming	2	110	27	62	56	56.4

[a]Number of adjudicated youth who participated in the survey and whose data were used to provide state-level estimates.

[b]Data for Connecticut and New Hampshire were not reported due to insufficient data to provide state rates.

[c]Excludes 14 facilities that could not be included in the state-level rate due to data disclosure restrictions. (See *Methodology* for description of state-level estimation procedures.)

[d]Youth were considered ineligible if they were mentally or physically incapacitated, admitted to the facility within 2 weeks prior to the data collection period, transferred or released after sample selection but before the data collection period, or excluded based on sub-sampling within the facility. (See *Methodology*.)

[e]Response rate accounts for different probabilities of selection among youth and the exclusion of interviews with extreme or inconsistent responses. (See *Methodology*.)

[f]Total differs from U.S. total because state-level estimates exclude interviews in 14 facilities due to data disclosure restrictions.

Source: Bureau of Justice Statistics, National Survey of Youth in Custody, 2012.

Percent of youth reporting sexual victimization, by type of incident and state, National Survey of Youth in Custody, 2012

	Percent of youth reporting any victimization by another youth			Percent of youth reporting any staff sexual misconduct		
		95%-confidence interval			95%-confidence interval	
State[a]	Weighted percent[b]	Lower bound	Upper bound	Weighted percent[b]	Lower bound	Upper bound
All states - U.S. total	2.5%	2.1%	3.0%	7.7%	7.0%	8.4%
Alabama	4.3	2.7	6.8	11.3	8.5	14.8
Alaska	1.7	0.9	3.2	2.6	1.5	4.4
Arizona	6.1	3.7	9.9	2.9	1.3	6.0
Arkansas	4.8	3.6	6.2	10.1	8.4	12.2
California	7.0	3.2	14.9	14.8	9.7	22.1
Colorado	4.1	2.9	5.7	5.5	4.3	7.0
Delaware	0.0	0.0	8.4	0.0	0.0	8.4
District of Columbia	0.0	0.0	8.5	0.0	0.0	8.5
Florida	1.0	0.5	1.8	4.5	3.1	6.6
Georgia	1.2	0.7	2.0	15.0	13.0	17.3
Hawaii	5.4	2.5	11.2	5.4	2.5	11.2
Idaho	1.6	1.0	2.6	2.2	1.5	3.2
Illinois	2.6	1.9	3.7	13.7	11.8	15.8
Indiana	1.6	1.1	2.4	8.7	7.2	10.3
Iowa	2.2	1.5	3.2	6.2	2.7	13.5
Kansas	3.4	2.3	5.1	13.5	10.9	16.7
Kentucky	0.5	0.2	1.2	3.4	2.5	4.7
Louisiana	0.9	0.2	3.6	4.3	2.9	6.3
Maine	2.6	1.2	5.4	3.7	2.0	6.7
Maryland	0.0	0.0	8.4	4.8	1.2	17.0
Massachusetts	0.0	0.0	2.2	0.0	0.0	2.2
Michigan	4.0	1.9	8.4	6.4	2.4	16.0
Minnesota	1.0	0.2	3.9	2.5	0.6	9.8
Mississippi	4.8	2.5	9.0	9.8	6.1	15.2
Missouri	1.8	1.4	2.4	2.4	1.9	3.0
Montana	8.7	2.9	23.1	8.7	2.9	23.1
Nebraska	4.2	0.9	17.7	0.0	0.0	10.4
Nevada	6.3	2.7	14.1	8.2	4.1	15.6
New Jersey	0.0	0.0	1.8	6.2	3.3	11.4
New Mexico	0.0	0.0	2.7	2.5	0.8	7.1
New York	0.0	0.0	9.0	0.0	0.0	9.0
North Carolina	0.0	0.0	2.4	4.2	2.1	8.3
North Dakota	5.5	3.1	9.6	1.8	0.7	4.7
Ohio	3.6	2.5	4.9	17.1	14.6	20.0
Oklahoma	9.0	2.3	29.0	9.4	4.7	17.8
Oregon	4.1	3.4	4.9	7.4	6.5	8.5
Pennsylvania	3.9	1.5	10.1	4.3	2.4	7.8
Rhode Island	0.0	0.0	4.9	5.1	1.9	12.8
South Carolina	4.3	3.0	6.1	17.0	14.4	19.8
South Dakota	5.4	1.5	18.3	0.0	0.0	6.8
Tennessee	0.0	0.0	2.4	13.0	8.5	19.5
Texas	2.0	1.4	2.8	10.2	8.4	12.4
Utah	6.8	3.6	12.4	5.3	2.8	9.6
Vermont	0.0	0.0	3.7	6.7	3.1	13.7
Virginia	2.8	1.0	7.6	8.4	5.3	13.2
Washington	2.9	1.2	6.6	4.6	2.4	8.7
West Virginia	1.8	1.1	2.9	12.7	10.7	14.9
Wisconsin	0.0	0.0	1.3	6.5	4.2	9.8
Wyoming	0.0	0.0	3.4	1.9	0.5	6.9

[a]Data for Connecticut and New Hampshire were not reported due to insufficient data to provide state rates. (See *Methodology* for estimation of state-level rates.)

[b]Weighted percentage of youth reporting one or more incidents of sexual victimization involving another youth or facility staff in the past 12 months or since admission to the facility, if less than 12 months.

Source: Bureau of Justice Statistics, National Survey of Youth in Custody, 2012.